and the Single Christian Girl

fighting for purity in a rom-com world

MARIAN JORDAN ELLIS

BETHANY HOUSE PUBLISHERS

a division of Baker Publishing Group
Minneapolis, Minnesota

© 2013 by Marian Jordan Ellis

Published by Bethany House Publishers
11400 Hampshire Avenue South
Bloomington, Minnesota 55438
www.bethanyhouse.com

Bethany House Publishers is a division of
Baker Publishing Group, Grand Rapids, Michigan

Printed in the United States of America

Library of Congress Cataloging-in-Publication Data
Jordan, Marian L.
   Sex and the single Christian girl : fighting for purity in a Rom-Com world / Marian Jordan Ellis.
      pages cm
   Includes bibliographical references.
   Summary: "Popular speaker offers young Christian women straight talk about sexuality and gives them tools to protect their purity"—Provided by publisher.
      ISBN 978-0-7642-1123-2 (pbk. : alk. paper)
      1. Sex—Religious aspects—Christianity. 2. Christian women—Sexual behavior. 3. Single people—Sexual behavior. I. Title.
   BT708.J665 2013
   241'.66408352—dc23   2013023252

Cover design by Connie Gabbert Design and Illustration LLC

Author is represented by DRS Agency

13   14   15   16   17   18   19   7   6   5   4   3   2   1

Contents

*This book is lovingly dedicated
to my husband, Justin.*

I did not know the meaning of the word *cherish*
until I met you. Thank you for cherishing me.
Words fail to express how grateful I am
to have you by my side
and to serve Jesus with you.

With you, I learned to "stand" against the evil one.
I know that God's best is worth fighting for,
worth praying for, and worth waiting for.

I love you.

Acknowledgments

I owe a great debt to the staff of Redeemed Girl Ministries for prayer, support, listening ears, extreme patience, and faithful counsel during the writing process. Thank you, Rebecca and Marianne; not only are you dear friends, but you are my ministry partners.

Thank you to my friends Angel and Catherine for sharing your time and talent to edit this book. Your gift is a treasure! I am also grateful for my friend Blake, who read the manuscript and was bold enough to tell me to start over. It is better because of your honesty.

I am forever grateful to the board of directors of Redeemed Girl Ministries for your wisdom, support, and prayers.

To my amazing family: Your faith is a rock. I'm humbled to be surrounded by such a great cloud of witnesses and know that your prayers move mountains!

To my agent, David Shepherd: You championed this book, and I am especially grateful for your persistence.

To the entire team at Baker Publishing Group and Bethany House Publishers: Your passion for truth and excellence continually inspires me. I am especially thankful to my editor, Tim Peterson, for partnering with me to see women set free by the grace and truth of Jesus Christ. This book would not be the same without your wise guidance and influence.

To my bonus boys, Brenden and Andrew: I cannot imagine life without you. It is an absolute privilege to be your stepmom. You are a daily reminder of God's goodness and faithfulness.

To my amazing husband, Justin: I love you. Not only do you model Christ's love to me, but you also lived the precepts of this book with me. Thank you for never settling for less than His best and for praying this work into existence. God's best is worth fighting for, worth waiting for, and worth praying for.

Introduction

a christian girl in a rom-com world

So what is it like to be a Christian woman in a rom-com world? For those of you who are unfamiliar with the term *rom-com*, it is slang for "romantic comedy." You know, the movies that you go see with girlfriends. The ones guys mockingly call "chick flicks." It is the genre that establishes which A-list leading man will, no doubt, end up on the cover of *People* magazine as the sexiest man alive. Romantic comedies make you laugh, cry, and run to the mall to buy what the leading lady wore.

A rom-com is that great comedic romp from *girl-likes-guy, guy-likes-girl* through *they-almost-don't-make-it-as-a-couple-yet-hilarity-ensues* to *at-the-last-possible-moment-they-finally-end-up-together-as-swelling-music-crescendos!*

At the final scene, we all tear up and glance sideways at each other to make sure we are not the only pathetic sap in the audience. We cast knowing looks to our girlfriends as we leave the theater while chatting and quoting our favorite one-liners. Which we will all memorize, of course!

Romantic comedies are the stuff a girls' night is made of. No boys. No makeup. No problem. All we need are flannel pajamas, a cuddly blanket, our favorite junk food, and anything starring Jennifer Aniston, Katherine Heigl, Kate Hudson, or Emma Stone. Rom-coms are just what they claim to be: both romantic and funny. Typically, we have a leading lady and a leading man who struggle through hilarious real-life relationship scenarios. This is part of the genius of the genre—we can insert ourselves into their drama.

However, unlike in real life, the man is often sensitive, verbose, and drop-dead gorgeous. He is the guy that has all of the one-liners our heart has yearned to hear from our own leading man. Except this guy does not stink after a workout—sweat simply accentuates his perfect abs. This guy does not forget your birthday or the song that was playing when you first met. This guy loves his dog—but not more than you. And the best thing about the rom-com guy is that he inexplicably has loads of money and a cool place to live without all the hassle of a real job to deal with.

Therefore, Mr. Rom-Com has oodles of time on his hands to bring you coffee, drop by your place of work with flowers, or cook you dinner while blasting his super cool tunes on his iPod. For some reason this guy usually has a penchant for jazz, which I still don't get, but it seems to give him immediate cool status. Oh, and it is very likely that he secretly paints or sketches on the side. Sigh.

Here's how Hollywood hooks us. Mr. Rom-Com will have a flaw—a fabulous flaw, that is. It usually just makes him more endearing to the audience, who is privy to the scenes that his leading lady does not get to see. For instance, he may not answer his phone when she calls. She then begins to suspect something is amiss. *Perhaps he is not so perfect after all. Perhaps,* she surmises, *there is another woman!* Unaware of the truth and feeling rejected, she accepts a date from a slick, not-so-sensitive real estate tycoon.

"But wait!" we scream from the other side of the silver screen, leaning forward in our sticky movie theater chairs. "He's not cheating—he is feeding orphans! Of course he leaves his phone tossed on the seat of his really cool vintage truck when he goes to visit little Susie with the limp. She needs his full-on attention!" Hooked on the suspense, we hold our breath in painful agony, hoping and wondering if the two star-crossed lovers will end up together.

And so, you see, this is the first problem for the single Christian woman living in a rom-com world. The romantic comedy formula hooks us and reels us in with near-perfect characters within very believable contexts. Our secret longings and desires are played like a fiddle, and we cast upon the leading lady our personal dreams for happily ever after.

But there's a catch. With its idyllic settings and loyal sexiest-man-alive characters, the rom-com sets us up for a serious crash; it's a fantasy. In a romantic comedy, everything wraps up in a beautiful little package in an hour and thirty minutes. But real life doesn't work that way. For one thing, there are never negative consequences for sex outside of marriage. In a rom-com world, everyone is happy, STD-free, and blissfully strolling off into the sunset.

Yes, ladies, for the single Christian woman who desires sexual purity, I believe this is one of our Enemy's secret weapons, which is launched through the stratosphere, wrapped in great lighting and good wardrobe, and set to the latest music by Norah Jones. The happy endings completely ignore the fact that these people (cheered on by us) slept together before they were married, and we actually pulled for them every clothes-tossing, table-clearing step of the way.

The power of the rom-com personally dawned on me one flannel-pj's-and-blanket night with a couple of my girlfriends. After the Cheetos and blueberry muffins were history, we discussed one of our all-time favorite movies, *The Holiday*, starring

Cameron Diaz and Jude Law. We love this movie. It delivers on so many levels: beautiful music, amazing scenery, quotable one-liners . . . and just a pinch of agony.

But here's the problem: I am a no-holds-barred, sold-out Christian woman. I love Jesus. I teach the Bible. I write Christian books for women. I speak on sexual purity and fight for it in my own life. And yet . . . and yet, I did not blink when Jude Law and Cameron Diaz had sex before they even knew each other's names.

For those of you who don't know the movie (*where on earth have you been?*), let me set up the scenario for you: Two women, each fresh from a breakup, want to take a "holiday" from their own lives. They stumble onto a website that offers a house-switch. One woman lives in a gorgeous home in Hollywood Hills, while the other lives in a quaint village in England. They switch. And romance and hilarity ensue.

Cameron Diaz's character, who is from Hollywood, finds herself in a village in England where there are no single men . . . or so she thinks. Cue Jude Law's character, who stumbles into her cottage looking rakishly handsome, if not terribly tipsy. Stone-cold-sober Cameron Diaz tries to shoo him away, but alas . . . they kiss and melt into the blankets together. Which, she assures us the next morning, *never* happens.

Pause.

Okay, I vaguely remember thinking this was a stupid move on her part because he could have been a serial killer. *But other than that,* no real clanging bells or screaming sirens went off in my mind. After all, Norah Jones was playing in the background, so I kinda knew he was no killer. Serial killers aren't set to Norah, right? Swaddled in rom-com perfection, their one-night stand seemed like no big deal.

What? No big deal? Who am I?

This thinking goes against everything I live for and believe. Yet I was absolutely engrossed in the story, hoping the two would live happily ever after!

This was the precise scenario that my friends and I began to discuss years later after we had each seen the movie a dozen times or so. Yes, ladies, a Christian woman can be bamboozled by the rom-com world. We can become so smitten with the feelings and one-liners emitted from the silver screen that we become desensitized to the immorality that has been wrapped up in a beautifully soft-lensed package.

How could I have missed this?

Now that we have established the power of the rom-com, I want to look more closely at why this good gal-bonding, heart-swooning genre makes it tough for Christian women to live out sexual purity. When the very thing you are fighting against in your own life is paraded as normal in your favorite flick, then the question of *why* purity matters gets super fuzzy when you are kissing your boyfriend. No wonder sexual purity is such a tough battle for Christian girls.

Recently, while on the road for a speaking event, I found myself with a few unplanned hours in Nashville before my flight home to Texas. So I called a friend who lives in the city to see if she had a few hours to spare to hang out until my flight. She is a worship leader and is often on the road, too. But to the surprise of both of us, she was in town and did have some free time! We met for coffee and caught up on ministry life, my recent marriage, and a few blind dates she'd recently had. Coffee progressed to shopping (duh), and while perusing a clearance sale, we started discussing the topic of this book.

I told her that I felt called to address the struggle that single Christian women face to remain pure in a romantic-comedy world. Standing in front of a full-length mirror with a latte in one hand and a killer new scarf in the other, my friend confessed: "It's getting to the point that I really struggle when I watch those kinds of movies. I have to fight to keep my thoughts pure and to resist temptation. As a single woman in my thirties, it's difficult to watch scenes that evoke desire for sex when I know that's not a possibility at this point in my life."

I applaud my friend's discernment, and recognize that her struggle is one common to many women. Her past before knowing Jesus was similar to my own, and she does not want to go back to a lifestyle of sin. So she is wise to keep her guard up to any way that Satan can creep in to deceive her and detour her into sexual sin.

I love a good romantic comedy as much as the next girl, but obviously, many of them are not edifying. Honestly, discernment is the key. I'm not writing this book in hopes that women will boycott movies or burn their favorite DVDs. That's not my style. My desire for this book is to expose the battle that rages around sexual purity.

* * *

Sex and the Single Christian Girl is for Jesus-loving girls living in a rom-com world. We may know what God says about sexual purity, but living it out proves to be a completely different story. It can be a tough world for a godly girl. We live in a culture that sells sex, promotes sex, and degrades sex, yet God calls His daughters to live as light in this darkness.

Today, sex is marketed as the norm for anyone, at any time, in any fashion. God's beautiful design for sex, to celebrate oneness and commitment, is now demeaned to nothing more than a cheap hookup. How did we get here? Christians today are inundated with a proliferation of messages that scream, "If it feels good, do it!" Contemporary television shows and movies portray couples sleeping together on date number one as the natural progression in a relationship.

In this book I will share my own struggle to fight for sexual purity. I will also include stories of other women who, after falling into sexual sin, are trying to live differently. While the topics in this book are direct and will expose our fears, insecurities, and vulnerabilities, I hope to encourage you with a God-sized vision of *why* sexual purity matters and equip you *with* the tools to live it out.

You may be reading this and thinking, *But, Marian, I want the fairy tale.* Stick with me. Our God writes the best love stories, and He does have a wonderful plan for your life. But as we will discover in subsequent chapters, there is an alternate script that Satan has for your life. This evil script provides a detour, where much more heart-wrenching scenes unfold.

Perhaps you've *Never Been Kissed*, or maybe you're the girl with *27 Dresses*, or maybe your life looks more like a scene from *Knocked Up*. Wherever you are on this journey, this book is for you. We all come from different backgrounds, but as Christians, we are all called to sexual purity. It is oh so easy for us to fall into a rom-com–induced haze of fuzzy morality and ebbing purity.

Trust me, my story before Christ was anything but pure. Like many young women of my generation, I viewed sex as "no big deal" and lived a very promiscuous lifestyle. Hoping for my own happy ending, I fell for all the lies concerning love and sex that I will discuss in upcoming chapters. So if I, by God's grace, can change, anyone can! The book you hold is written from the perspective of a woman who loves Jesus, who was transformed by grace, and who fought for sexual purity. While it was not easy, I can say with my whole heart that purity was worth fighting for! These are lessons that I learned on the battlefield, and I hope this book will inform you, challenge you, and empower you to win your own battle for sexual purity in a rom-com world.

I want the fairy tale.

~ Vivian Ward (Julia Roberts)
in *Pretty Woman*

1

Worth Fighting For

God created marriage as a living, breathing portrait laid out
before the eyes of the world so that they might see the story
of the ages. A love story, set in the midst of desperate times.
It is a story of redemption, a story of healing; it is a story of
love. God gives us marriage to illustrate His heart toward us.

—*Love and War* by John and Stasi Eldredge

Raw, unfiltered emotion hit me like a mighty rushing wind. As
I took my first steps to walk down the aisle on my father's
arm, the sheer intensity of the moment ripped through me. I was
completely undone. Just as wind precedes rain, the tears quickly
began to fall. When I say tears, I do mean sobs. Yes, I full-on
ugly-cried all the way down the aisle on my wedding day. Not
exactly what one would want in photos that last a lifetime. Yet
at thirty-eight years old, it should not surprise anyone that I shed
a few tears—but the full extent of the crying bears explanation.

First, by far the easiest emotion to explain was my pure, un-
bridled joy. Like rain on a sunny day, tears mingled with radiance.

Later, when asked by a five-year-old if I was crying because I was sad, I said, "Oh no, that was the happiest day of my life." My joy was uncontainable, and it seeped out of every pore and tear duct of my body.

Gratitude hit me next. For starters, after months of planning, I finally saw my family's old barn transformed into a cathedral. One word: breathtaking. I was beyond thankful to friends and family who worked tirelessly to plan and execute my dream wedding. Theirs was a labor of love, and I its humbled recipient. Then gratefulness hit me once again as we entered and I saw beloved faces—friends and family who traveled from across the country to show their support and join our celebration. With each face, fresh tears. Their support was a gift, just like God's grace—unmerited.

Primarily, I found myself overwhelmed with sheer thankfulness to my loving heavenly Father, whose sovereign goodness and perfect plan were arranged that day. Grasping the bigger story, I realized that my heavenly Father loved me too much to let me settle for less than His best. Every broken heart and all those years of waiting were a gift. He loved me enough to allow me to wait, long past *my* timetable, for His time and for His man. My heavenly Father wanted His best for me, and every *no* along the way was His *yes* to the best.

Then I saw him, my groom. He stood, eyes beaming with his trademark beautiful smile, and he watched me, with his own tears, as I walked toward him. In that moment, everyone else disappeared. I can't tell you how much I love this man. At this point, words just fall flat. He is by far the kindest, most Christlike man I've ever met. But while I was extremely grateful for the gift that Justin is, when I saw his face, a new emotion unleashed. Relief.

Relief? This may seem a strange emotion for a bride to feel on her wedding day, but honestly, I can't think of a better way to express the ultimate source of my tears. For it was when I looked into his eyes, and the relief washed over me, that the true sobs broke forth. We've all witnessed this kind of emotion before. Perhaps you've seen it in a movie, or in a touching airport reunion. It's that moment when the war ends, the troops come home, and the loved ones race into each other's arms. Those aren't tears of sorrow; they're tears bursting forth from a well called relief. The war . . . it was finally over. *Sweet relief.*

In many ways, my single years were a type of war zone. Sure, I battled through heartbreaks and loneliness. But my true weariness was from years of standing against an invisible Enemy who despises God's glory and seeks to detour Christians away from God's good and perfect will. All those years Satan tempted me to settle, to follow the world's ways, to forsake the desire of my heart to be cherished, and mostly, to forsake my Jesus. My single years were a faith walk—to trust in God's promises and to resist the lies and schemes of the Enemy. So when I saw Justin's face, with knowing looks we said to each other, "We made it." I knew in that moment that God's best was worth fighting for. The battle over sexual purity and the fight to resist our Enemy was more than worth it. No shame. No regret. Robed in white. Ready. Enveloped in peace. Sweet relief flooded my heart.

While dear friends sang my favorite hymn, "Fairest Lord Jesus," we arrived at the altar for my father to give my hand to my groom. In that moment I felt the powerful presence of God rest on that Texas hilltop. Then, looking up, I saw it. Positioned high above the altar, at the top of the barn and the central point of the ceremony, was the most gorgeous cross of white flowers— the symbol of God's perfect love. It was a reminder of my Jesus, my first love, who mercifully died to redeem my life, whose love transformed me, and without whom I never would have stood at that altar.

Justin then accepted my hand from my father, pulled me to his side, placed a kiss on my temple, and whispered, "You are my treasure." As the worship team transitioned to the Doxology and sang, "Praise God from whom all blessings flow," a powerful rushing wind whipped through, lifting my veil to the heavens.

We were standing on holy ground.

It was a reminder from the Lord—marriage is sacred. And as our God was lifted high in praise, Jesus graced us with the outpouring of His Spirit. In response to His presence, I lifted my bouquet high in praise and wept sweet tears of worship to my God.

Purity

I do not share the story of my wedding day to convey that my experience is the end goal for women who pursue sexual purity. It doesn't matter if we are married or single. Whatever season of life we find ourselves in, we share a common purpose and a common Enemy. One season is not more honorable or less difficult than the other. Married women are in a battle for purity just as much as single women. We live in a world filled with darkness at every turn, and our hearts and minds are continually under assault. A wedding ring does not make a woman immune to spiritual darkness. What I hoped to communicate to the best of my ability was the sheer relief that washed over me as I stood at that altar and realized . . . Satan didn't win!

Today, I still fight an invisible Enemy, whose desire is to "steal and kill and destroy" (John 10:10). Spiritual warfare did not end on my wedding day. What I hope to convey in this book is the particular brand of warfare a single Christian woman faces who seeks to honor God with her body by remaining sexually pure.

Through my many years as a single woman, I fought lies, temptations, fears, and worldly influences. Standing against these pressures was not easy. The battle for purity was a long and hard-fought endeavor for one reason—the glory of His name! From the time I fell in love with Jesus, God's glory was the desire of my soul. The choice to fight was birthed out of a deep love for God.

Somewhere along the way, it clicked. I stopped trying to remain sexually pure just to follow a rule or to "save myself for my future husband." As a single woman in her thirties, I didn't know if there would be a "future husband." A far more compelling reason gripped my heart. I wanted to offer my body, my whole self, to the Lord as a living act of worship. As the apostle Paul so eloquently stated in Philippians:

> But whatever were gains to me I now consider loss for the sake of Christ. What is more, I consider everything a loss because of the surpassing worth of knowing Christ Jesus my Lord, for whose sake I have lost all things. I consider them garbage, that I may gain Christ and be found in him, not having a righteousness of my own that comes from the law, but that which is through faith in Christ—the righteousness that comes from God on the basis of faith. I want to know Christ—yes, to know the power of his resurrection and participation in his sufferings, becoming like him in his death, and so, somehow, attaining to the resurrection from the dead.
>
> Not that I have already obtained all this, or have already arrived at my goal, but I press on to take hold of that for which Christ Jesus took hold of me. Brothers and sisters, I do not consider myself yet to have taken hold of it. But one thing I do: Forgetting what is behind and straining toward what is ahead, I press on toward the goal to win the prize for which God has called me heavenward in Christ Jesus.
>
> Philippians 3:7–14

I love that phrase, "the surpassing worth of knowing Christ Jesus my Lord." As I set out to write a book for Christian women on sexual purity, one of the most difficult aspects is convincing anyone that purity is worth fighting for. What compels someone to resist, to stand, and to fight must come from a place deep within that wants something better. My "something better" is and was

Jesus. Throughout this book, I'm going to be brutally honest and confess I struggled. Sexual purity was tough, but what kept me fighting was my desire to honor Christ. I wanted to stand before Him unashamed. As Paul said:

> I eagerly expect and hope that I will in no way be ashamed, but will have sufficient courage so that now as always Christ will be exalted in my body, whether by life or by death. For to me, to live is Christ and to die is gain.
>
> Philippians 1:20–21

Fairest Lord Jesus

Purity is not defined by whether we are married or single or if we are in a relationship or not. Purity is about exalting Jesus to the watching world as better. I was single until my late thirties and knew Jesus as my all in all—my strength, my light, my Lord, my provider, my protector, my comforter, my husband, and my best friend. My single season was a gift—one that I will always treasure. I desired marriage, but I knew the Lord ordained my season of singleness, and I experienced great joy and purpose in His will for my life.

When the Lord placed marriage on my heart and I began earnestly praying for my future husband, it wasn't because I was suddenly graduating from singleness to marriage—as if singleness were a lesser calling. Not at all! God's plan was unfolding and I was simply walking in His will. Today, in this new season God has ordained for me, I can praise and proclaim that Jesus is still my all in all. Friends, our heavenly Father writes the best stories. He has a unique plan for each of us, but a woman who is walking in His will (married or single) can glorify Jesus with her purity in whatever season or stage of life.

Søren Kierkegaard said, "Purity of heart is to will one thing." For the single Christian woman who loves Jesus, her "one thing" is

Christ himself. The glory of Christ becomes our supreme purpose and passion. Therefore, the pursuit of sexual purity is, in fact, the pursuit of Jesus—not the pursuit of a man or marriage. Purity of body and soul is about one thing: a woman's heart being so consumed with the glory of God that she will fight to resist a real and present Enemy who seeks to pull her away from her First Love. Holiness is a life set apart to God; therefore, purity is not defined simply by a set of moral rules but as a life fully devoted to Jesus and His glory.

In the Bible, men and women were often consecrated unto the Lord. *Consecration* simply means to be "set apart" unto God. To be set apart or consecrated to God means to be wholly His. You may be reading this book and deeply desire marriage, or you may be reading and feel called to singleness for the rest of your life. Whatever the future holds, single or married, none of us really knows, but we can begin today by fully devoting ourselves to Jesus. Consecration is the heartbeat of a woman who flat-out loves Jesus. She is motivated by more than just a white dress on a wedding day. She sees herself as belonging to the Lord; therefore, the end goal of sexual purity is not marriage but her devotion to Christ.

For this reason, I chose to walk down the aisle to my favorite hymn, "Fairest Lord Jesus." More than beautiful flowers or Pinterest-worthy decorations, I wanted Jesus lifted high and honored. I wanted to declare—without question—that He is my first love. Originally, I chose this hymn simply because it is a favorite, but reflecting on the words and the significance of the moment, I now see a beautiful connection between our passion for Christ and our pursuit of purity:

> *Fairest Lord Jesus, ruler of all nature,*
> *O thou of God and man the Son,*
> *Thee will I cherish, Thee will I honor,*
> *thou, my soul's glory, joy, and crown.*

A passionate pursuit of God's glory becomes the driving ambition of a woman's heart when Jesus is our "soul's glory, joy, and crown." The choice to live a holy and pure life finds its origin in our love for Him. There were many nights when Justin and I were dating that this proved true.

At the outset of our relationship, we openly discussed our expectations and the desire to remain sexually pure. We set clear boundaries concerning our physical limits and candidly discussed our pasts and weaknesses. We shared the same vision concerning God's design for sex and marriage, and knew we wanted to protect and honor our future marriage. All this to say, our hearts were in the right place and we both wanted to please God. And yet we still struggled.

Typically, we would find ourselves weak to temptation late at night, when it was time for us to leave each other and return to our separate houses. The tempting voices would begin to whisper, "Just stay the night. You will be fine. You won't do anything." (Yeah, right!) Those voices in my head that justified and minimized sin would grow louder. As the minutes clicked by, we both knew we were standing at temptation's doorstep and that cracking open the door would welcome in stronger ones. Sure, we would have loved to stay together longer, but we both knew that would lead us into even more temptation.

In those moments we would look at each other and say, "I love you, but I love Jesus more. For that reason, I'm going home." Our love for God conquered and was our power to resist Satan. Girls, I'll be the first to admit that the choice to say no to temptation was never easy, but when we stood before each other on our wedding day, I knew the wait was worth it.

A single Christian woman who loves Jesus Christ does indeed live in a war zone. Each step I took before walking down that aisle was a battle with my own flesh that wanted to sin, but also with an invisible Enemy who desired to detour me from God's best. The battle still continues on this side of marriage, but the unique battle that single Christian women face is the one that I know must be addressed—I want to equip my sisters in Christ for victory.

First, as noted, purity is birthed out of a passionate love for Jesus. Second, purity is rooted in knowing and believing your identity in Christ. These are two essentials for victory—and they are both beautifully conveyed in a word that I finally grasped the meaning of on my wedding day: *cherish*.

*Listen, girls. If you don't respect yourself,
how do you expect others to respect you?*

~ Mike O'Donnell (Zac Efron)
in *17 Again*

2

Cherish

> Beware how you give your heart.
>
> —Jane Austen,
> *Northanger Abbey*

Chick flicks capture the frenzy, and newsstands are littered with the evidence: Some women are flat-out wedding crazy. The wedding industry is a billion-dollar business. Girls are absolutely *obsessed* with being a bride. So much so that there are now television shows, magazines, professional planners, stylists, designers, workout DVDs, trade shows, photographers, and personal wedding websites all clamoring to deliver a girl her "dream wedding."

People magazine frequently features the most over-the-top celebrity weddings, only adding fuel to the ever-growing fire. Extravagance is the new normal. Girls obsess over creating the perfect invitations—from scratch. And making flower arrangements out of wildflowers. And creating the perfect menu of locally grown produce. And picking paint chips to get the perfect color palate. Bridal magazines are like crack to women who will starve, scrimp, and scrap in pursuit of their perfect day.

I came across a popular online discussion forum that posted this question: "Why are women obsessed with weddings?" The forum was flooded with thread after thread of comments. While people are perplexed by the immense allure of all-things-bridal, few provided an answer to explain the fixation. Looking past the occasional bridezilla who just craves the spotlight, I believe this desire in most girls points to an innate, God-given desire for covenant love. After all, isn't that what the ring on the left hand is meant to symbolize?

Intrinsic to a woman's nature is the longing for covenant love. There's a reason women flock to romantic comedies and little girls dress up as their favorite fairy-tale princesses—our souls were fashioned by a God who loves us sacrificially, who says we are worth fighting for. This love story is inscribed upon our very souls. For so many women, a wedding is about this fairy tale coming to life.

Strip away the glitz and glamour, and a wedding is about one thing: a man and a woman standing before God, binding their lives together with holy vows. The altar, the aisle, the witnesses, and the rings all point to a covenant. Deep within the heart of a woman, she desires to be chosen—for someone to love, honor, and cherish her . . . till death do they part.

Traditional wedding vows contain three simple yet profoundly beautiful tokens of devotion: The groom stands before God and witnesses at an altar—biblically known as a place of sacrifice— and commits to lay down his life in order to love, honor, and cherish his bride. This vow stands as a picture to the watching world of what Christ did for His bride, the church. The Christian wedding vow is based in Scripture, where God reveals the mystery that Jesus' sacrificial love is the model for Christian marriage.

Husbands, love your wives, just as Christ also loved the church
and gave Himself up for her, so that He might sanctify her, having cleansed her by the washing of water with the word, that He
might present to Himself the church in all her glory, having no
spot or wrinkle or any such thing; but that she would be holy
and blameless. So husbands ought also to love their own wives
as their own bodies. He who loves his own wife loves himself; for
no one ever hated his own flesh, but nourishes and cherishes it,
just as Christ also does the church, because we are members of
His body. For this reason a man shall leave his father and mother
and shall be joined to his wife, and the two shall become one
flesh. This mystery is great; but I am speaking with reference to
Christ and the church.

Ephesians 5:25–32 NASB

"Love, honor, and cherish . . ." *Cherish* is hands down my favorite word of the trio. Perhaps I like it because it is not abused and
overused like its sister word, *love*. Nowadays people claim to fall in
and out of love within the span of a thirty-minute reality TV show.
The word *cherish*, on the other hand, still has weight. It stands apart
as a word picture of true love in action. To cherish something is
to hold it in honor and to place high value upon it. Cherish is love
wearing work boots. This love is not the run-of-the-mill emotional
love of chick-flick lore, but the love that seeks the best for the other,
the covenant-keeping love that puts work behind the words. This is
the high and holy calling that the Lord God places on a man who
would be entrusted with one of His daughters.

A recent event taught me a great deal about the intrinsic connection between *cherish* and *value*. A week after my wedding,
I packed up all my belongings to move from Houston to San
Antonio to begin my new life with my husband. The wedding
festivities now behind us, it was time to begin our real dance
as husband and wife. Movers arrived, loaded box after box of
my former single-girl life into a truck, and shipped it off to a

33

storage unit. This move was huge. My whole life was swaddled in Bubble Wrap. After years of living solo, I'd collected many treasures—items that were especially valuable to me, ones I took special care to protect.

These were not valuable in the materialistic sense of the word, but treasures that held a special place in my heart. Over the years, as I've traveled the world in ministry, I've collected special objects that remind me of a particular place, person, or experience. While packing these items, I carefully wrapped each one before placing it into a box. Each box was then meticulously marked: *Fragile: Handle with care. Breakable. Do not crush.* I took this precaution because these objects were cherished.

Think of your own home.

What do you cherish?

Why is it a treasure to you?

Why is it valuable or sentimental?

Perhaps a family heirloom comes to mind. The object itself may be worthless to someone else, but to you it is a treasure. That is the meaning of *cherished.* Something is valued because it points to something greater. For example, my grandmother's teacup is not just a piece of china. No, it points to something greater, to someone I dearly loved.

A few weeks passed and we opened the storage unit to begin the painstaking process of unpacking. Once inside, I discovered the boxes that I had carefully marked *Fragile: Handle with care* were crushed. As I unpacked and surveyed the damage done from ignored instructions, I sensed God speaking a word to my heart.

"Marian, this is exactly how a generation of my daughters willingly treat themselves. They are my treasures that I paid the highest price to redeem. I cherish them, yet they ignore my instructions, and they are crushed. My heart breaks for their tears, their shame, and their brokenness. I long for them to be treated like treasures, yet they settle for so much less than my best."

Taking inventory of the destruction, I saw the parallels oh so clearly. We are cherished by God because we, too, point to something greater—we point to His Son, Jesus, who paid the ultimate price to redeem us.

> It was not with perishable things such as silver or gold that you were redeemed from the empty way of life handed down to you from your ancestors, but with the precious blood of Christ, a lamb without blemish or defect. He was chosen before the creation of the world, but was revealed in these last times for your sake.
>
> 1 Peter 1:18–20

Ladies, please don't miss the words "for your sake." Sexual purity begins with understanding the heart of God; He loves you, He desires His best for you, and He defines your value. God, who is the ultimate authority, has spoken. You are more valuable than silver or gold, for He paid the highest possible price to rescue you. When He speaks a commandment to you, He does so to Bubble Wrap His treasure in order to protect you.

This is the heart of our heavenly Father, who longs for us to be cherished. He expects you to be honored. He expects your purity to be guarded. Most important, your heavenly Father expects a man to love you as Christ loves the church.

May I ask a tough question?

Do you expect the same for yourself?

Just as those movers failed to heed my instructions, and as a result my belongings were destroyed, when we ignore God's instructions concerning love, dating, and marriage, we, too, are crushed.

Sexual purity springs forth from a woman's heart when she knows and believes that she is cherished—a highly valued daughter of God who is worth fighting for. But let's be honest. In the world we live in, women don't often see themselves as "cherished" or "priceless treasures," nor do they see sex as sacred. But why?

Our culture's base and degraded view of sex is truly a reflection of how our culture has dismissed God. And right along with the debased view of sex is a debased view of humanity.

Sex is cheap in our culture for many reasons, but one of the primary reasons is that we've failed to see ourselves as people made in the image of God. Many Christians even fail to recall that they are the temples of the living God and that His Spirit dwells in them.

We are the creation of a beautiful and loving God. When we fail to see Him rightly, we fail to see ourselves rightly. Sex only becomes sacred again when we see our bodies as sacred. When I started to see God for who He is, then and only then could I begin to see myself for who He says that I am. We behave how we believe. We live out the truth that resides in our innermost being. So when a woman sees herself as God sees her—cherished—she will align her life to that truth. Her choices reflect her core identity.

Recently I had a conversation with a mother sick with worry. Her daughter is in college and is in love. She struggles with insecurity, although you'd never know it by looking at her. She is smart, beautiful, and gifted. She professes faith in Jesus, yet she continually settles for guys who do not share her love for Christ.

She is a girl who finds her worth in a guy. Over and over again, her heart is broken. Her current boyfriend doesn't treat her with very much love or respect. She isn't his priority. He doesn't honor her purity. He consistently puts himself first. Yet she chooses to stay with him. Her mom finally broke down and said to her, "You love him, but he doesn't cherish you. You deserve someone who will treat you as God wants you to be treated." I'm sure those words were hard for her to hear, but they were oh so needed. Sadly, this girl is not alone. I've met countless women who settle for less than God's best because deep down, they don't believe they are cherished—or worth dying for.

Worth Dying For

Move over, Nicholas Sparks, your books don't hold a candle to the greatest love story of all time, the Gospel. The Gospel is God's love story. Much like a knight in shining armor, Jesus left the splendor of heaven and stepped into our mess. Why? To fight for us.

Unlike in fairy tales, Jesus didn't slay the dragon, He allowed the dragon to inflict on Him the most horrific death ever invented—crucifixion. And for three full, horrific days, it seemed like darkness won. But one bright Sunday morning the tomb was found vacant and the graveclothes empty. Jesus overcame death, bringing new life to His love.

Why does this matter? Let this truth resonate deep inside your soul:

There was a choice; Jesus made it.

There was a burden; Jesus took it.

There was a problem; Jesus solved it.

Jesus willingly went to the cross to die . . . *for you.* He experienced unbelievable suffering and shame all with one purpose in mind: to rescue you. As Ephesians 5:25 plainly states, "Husbands, love your wives, just as Christ loved the church and gave himself up for her." That's you and that's me—the bride of Christ. He "gave himself up" for us. Jesus' sacrificial love defines the word *cherished* and stands as God's expectation for how a man should treat one of His daughters. Stop and really read that Scripture. Pause. Believe. The God of the universe said with outstretched arms that you were "worth dying for." Believing this truth transforms everything . . .

how you see yourself,

how you treat yourself,

how you view purity,

how you date,

and most important, whom you marry.

I should know, because God's love story, the Gospel, transformed everything about me.

Redeemed Girl

Before Christ redeemed me, I was a young woman living in the party scene, searching for love in the empty world of hookups. I didn't see myself as cherished. My life in college and my early twenties was such a far cry from the holy ground of my wedding day. Back then I masked my pain and emptiness with alcohol—pretending to myself and to others that I was okay. In reality, my soul was a gaping hole aching to be filled. I tried everything—substances, attention, sex, shopping, accolades . . . I tried them all. My problem was one common to the human condition—no one could fill the emptiness in my soul that longed for love.

Until I met Jesus, that is.

Jesus. Oh, how I love Him. By reconciling us to God the Father through His sacrificial death, He rescued us from that horrible emptiness and insecurity of life without Him. As C. S. Lewis so brilliantly observed:

> God made us: invented us as a man invents an engine. A car is made to run on petrol, and it would not run properly on anything else. Now God designed the human machine to run on Himself. He Himself is the fuel our spirits were designed to burn, or the food our spirits were designed to feed on. There is no other. That is why it is just no good asking God to make us happy in our own way without bothering about religion. God cannot give us a happiness and peace apart from Himself, because it is not there.[1]

When we are finally reconciled to our life source, our frantic search for love and for an identity is answered. We can stop searching. In relationship with Jesus, our heart's hunger for love is met. Not only does Jesus forgive us, but He also heals us of all the self-inflicted pain accumulated in vainly searching for love apart from Him. But most important, he transforms us by His love—a love that says we are *worth dying for.*

As the truth of the Gospel sank deep into my soul, I began to see myself as God sees me: *cherished.* I began to define my worth as He defines me: *worth dying for.* Romans 12:2 states that we should not "conform to the pattern of this world, but be transformed by the renewing of your mind." A renewed mind is one that is aligned with God's truth and not conformed to Satan's lies. When my mind began to truly believe those three powerful words, my life was radically transformed as a result. This revelation brought transformation:

- I no longer saw God's commandments concerning sex and marriage as a prohibition, but as His loving protection.
- I no longer thought of sexual purity as a rule, but as a desired virtue.
- I no longer was attracted to the guys who treated girls like commodities, but was now attracted to men of character who modeled Jesus' humility and self-sacrifice.
- I no longer saw my body as something to use to gain a guy's attention; I now viewed it as God's holy temple.

Do you see it? Those three words—*worth dying for*—change everything! As we've discovered, Jesus' sacrificial love is the standard to which our heavenly Father calls men. But is it our standard? Do we expect the men of our generation to treat us as Christ would? I daresay the majority of women I've counseled do not.

- Many women feel ashamed if they actually expect a commitment.
- Most have abandoned their true desire to be treasured and have instead fallen in step with a culture that expects girls to act cheap instead of cherished.

- Many lie to themselves and say they are content "just hanging out," all the while fearfully hiding their true desire for a commitment based on a covenant.

- Some use alcohol and drugs to silence the hurt in their soul from sexual sin and dismiss their God-given value by embracing our culture's attitude toward casual sex.

- Others are maintaining purity but have simply given up hope that God's best is even a viable option, lamenting that there just aren't any good men out there anymore.

It's a Tough World

In a culture where *virgin* is deemed a dirty word, it is rare that a young woman today would see her purity as worth fighting for. Sadly, women are seduced into believing a lie, one that says they shouldn't expect a guy to honor them and treat them as Christ would treat His bride, like a *treasure*.

Long gone are the days when fathers would sit potential suitors down for "the talk" before granting permission to court their daughters; therefore, young women today are often left unprotected. This lack of protection is coupled with a culture that brainwashes women to view themselves as cheap and usable. Girls raised in non-Christian homes are not the only ones to believe this lie. The onslaught has reached the front steps, living rooms, and backseats of Christian families nationwide.

The epidemic of teen pregnancy, STDs, and degradation of virtue is now the norm in the church house as well as the sorority house. This brainwashing has led to a sacrifice of purity and a flushing away of courtship, virtue, and the hope of a marriage built on godly principles and sacrificial love.

Single Christian women in the dating world have a fight on their hands. Teenagers, college students, and single professional women of all ages are constantly imprinted with the message of worldly pleasure and carnal expectations. Frankly, men have no reason to pursue a woman who has absolutely no idea she is worth the pursuit, worth the effort, *worth fighting for.*

It's a tough world for a godly girl.

This book is written from one woman to another, because I've been there. I understand the fears and longings particular to a woman's heart. I understand the battles we face with insecurity and how this war within can lead us to disastrous choices. I understand the pressure to conform to a culture that does not cherish women. I understand the years of waiting for God's best and how tempting it is to lose hope. I understand the battle with temptation and how easily the sin-nature will settle for cheap rather than cherished.

Girls, I get it. . . . I've been there. I also know we have a choice:

- A choice to believe God's definition of our value and worth.
- A choice to align our lives with God's beautiful design concerning love, marriage, and sexual purity.
- A choice to say no to temptation in order to say yes to God's best.
- A choice to stand against an invisible Enemy who seeks to destroy us.

In a tsunami of smut, how does a woman keep her way pure? By understanding God's jealous love for His daughters, we will learn to align our thinking and self-appraisals to the standard of God's truth. With minds renewed by God's Word, we can better discern the lies that hold us captive. As a result, new thinking will lead to new behavior. With renewed minds, we will discover that not only are we *worth dying for*, but once this truth is firmly established, we will discover that God's best is worth fighting for.

I have many goals in writing this book, but more than anything else, I pray the Lord reveals to your heart that you are cherished.

You may be fifteen or you may be fifty—this truth is needed for women of all ages. Once you comprehend your true identity in Christ, I pray you will never settle for less than His best. Sure, it is a tough world out there. But I know God's best is available and His promises are true. But we must choose to believe.

Are you willing to say no to the detours that will come your way?

Are you willing to wait for His best?

Are you willing to resist the temptations along the way?

If you are tired of settling for less than God's best, I want to invite you to pick up your sword and join me in the beautiful fight.

Don't you sometimes wonder if it's worth all this? I mean what you're fighting for.

~ Rick Blaine (Humphrey Bogart)
in *Casablanca*

3

The War Against the Soul

The greatest trick the devil ever pulled was convincing the world he doesn't exist.

—Charles Baudelaire

Ignorance is not bliss; it proves to be downright dangerous.

How could I have been so naïve? Looking back now, I realize that I was a girl in the midst of a cosmic war and didn't even know I was in a fistfight. For in my state of blissful ignorance, I came extremely close to losing the battle, until by God's grace I woke up, then wised up and started to fight.

This admission proves totally embarrassing to confess, but in my state of ignorance concerning spiritual warfare and the blissful glee that happens when a girl falls in love with her future husband, I almost fell right into Satan's trap. What trap, you ask? Oh, the Enemy's little ol' web of deceitful lies and temptations designed to lure me into sexual sin that would sow seeds of destruction in my life and my future marriage.

Honestly, I should not have been so naïve. As I said before, my life before I fell in love with Jesus was a sad tale of hookups and heartbreaks, but at age twenty-five, I experienced radical redemption. To *redeem* means to buy something back or to restore something. This is precisely what Jesus did in my life. I am a redeemed girl! He rescued me from the darkness of a life without Him, a life marred by sexual sin and the brokenness that resulted. After God redeemed me, He began the beautiful process of transformation: cleansing, healing, restoring—Jesus set me free.

Restoring my innocence.

Transforming my thoughts.

Healing my soul.

Setting me free.

The Bible says, "If anyone is in Christ, he is a new creation" (2 Corinthians 5:17 ESV). This is my story. Jesus literally made all things new.

One of the by-products of our salvation is the new heart we receive when we place faith in Jesus Christ. (See Ezekiel 36:26–27.) We have new desires. Whereas before Christ, we wanted to live only for ourselves and satisfy our old sinful nature, now *in* Christ we have living in us the Spirit of God, who eagerly desires to honor Jesus.

During my years of transformation, I fell head over heels in love with Him. And guess what? The more I loved Him, the more I longed to live a life of purity. This is the beautiful secret to a holy life. Love motivates obedience. I wanted to live a life that brought glory to my Redeemer. More than anything, I wanted to wait for God's best, to remain sexually pure until my wedding day, and to honor my First Love—Jesus.

So how could I of all people be surprised at the war over sexual purity? After all, I am a Bible teacher and I speak to women across the nation about God's design for sex. It's not like I didn't know the repeated warnings from Scripture about temptation. "If you think you are standing firm, be careful that you don't fall! No temptation has overtaken you except what is common to mankind" (1 Corinthians 10:12–13).

Sure, I was sexually active before I committed my life to Christ. But I naïvely assumed that once I surrendered my life to Jesus, my struggle with sexual temptation would be behind me. While I was a Christ-follower for over a decade when I met my husband, I can honestly say that I had not yet experienced the absolute war surrounding sexual purity to the degree that I did until we were dating and engaged.

I knew temptation is a reality all believers face, but honestly, I just assumed that if I loved Jesus and wanted to walk in purity, then I would be fine. My heart desired to remain sexually pure for my husband and for the glory of God. Therefore, I assumed my good intentions would carry me through to my wedding day. I quickly learned that good intentions aren't always good enough. I didn't realize the sheer power of temptation. I didn't realize that Satan's schemes are tactical. He knew my insecurities, he knew my fears, and he knew my weaknesses. Unbeknownst to me, I was facing a strategic move by a cunning Enemy who seeks "to steal and kill and destroy" (John 10:10), and who will use any means or method to accomplish his mission.

I knew about spiritual warfare, but I assumed that those battles were fought on the mission field, in places far, far away. Therefore, I found myself unprepared and ill equipped for the battle I would face when falling in love and taking steps toward marriage.

Jesus didn't call Satan the Father of Lies just for kicks. This title clearly describes our Enemy's primary weapons: lies, schemes, deception. He's crafty. So much so that I didn't even know he was in operation. I was caught off guard by the onslaught of lies strategically aimed at my insecurities and fears. These were not just your run-of-the-mill temptations. I can only describe this season as a full-on attack. I hate to sound dramatic, but the temptations came on so forcefully strong—like a tornado emerging on a clear spring day—that I know something out of the ordinary was operating.

Fears mingled with lies swirled and hurled against my resistance as the Enemy tempted me to sin and forsake God's commands concerning sexual purity. Little did I know at the time the degree to which our Enemy hates marriage, holiness, and God's glory. Nor did I comprehend the lengths to which he will go to detour Christians from experiencing the glorious blessings that follow obedience. As Robert Jeffress rightly observes:

> As a Christian, you are in the cross hairs of the Enemy's artillery. Whether you believe you are living in the middle of a cosmic war between God and Satan is immaterial to the devil. In fact, he prefers that you stay oblivious to the real battle raging in the universe and to your place in the battle. Like any combatant, Satan always operates more efficiently in the darkness than in the light. He has placed a giant X on your back and has marked you for destruction. The less aware you are of his goal, the more certain he is of success. Regardless of your level of awareness, you do have an Enemy intent on destroying you.[1]

Blissfully in love, happily humming Taylor Swift, I was absolutely unaware that I was positioned squarely in the Enemy's cross hairs.

The Love Drug

When I was a single Christian woman in my mid-twenties and early thirties, without any prospect of a husband on the horizon, I was far removed from the powerful force of what I call the "love drug"—the drug that numbs senses and causes a normal

Jesus-loving woman to walk around in a fuzzy haze. I was immune to the force . . . until I met "the one."

I fell in love with the most amazing man. I'll never forget when the proverbial shot pricked my arm and the love drug oozed throughout my entire being. We were sitting at dinner and Justin shared with me his love for Jesus and how the Lord was his only strength through an extremely tough season of life. As he expressed his passion for Jesus, a tear rolled down his cheek.

Right then I swooned. Girls, I was a goner.

Here was the one that I'd prayed and waited for (and secretly feared didn't really exist). Sitting beside me was the man who I would learn during our dating relationship was God's perfect will for my life. Over the months our love grew, and my longing to be his wife increased daily. Since I'd never known love of this nature, I wasn't prepared for the intensity with which my entire being would long to be one with him.

When you are wrapped in the fuzzy bubble of infatuation, it proves hard to remember that you are living in a war zone. As months passed and passions heightened, I found myself increasingly drawn to this man I loved. Honestly, my flesh (the old sinful nature) wanted to sin. At this point in our dating relationship, an intense battle for my mind and my will truly began. Like a battle-weary soldier, it would have been so easy to wave the white flag and surrender to defeat. I knew I had a choice: Indulge my flesh or resist my Enemy.

All of these emotions and longings are good—wonderful, in fact. They are God-given gifts to move us toward the covenant of marriage. But there was a choice before us each day of courtship—would we wait?

Would I choose to wait for God's best while my flesh screamed, "Just do it"?

Would I choose to resist while my Enemy whispered, "It's no big deal"?

Would I choose to stand against a culture that mocks purity as antiquated?

Would I choose to deal with my own insecurities and heart issues that were making me vulnerable to Satan's lies?

Let me be clear: Justin honored my purity. Thankfully, he was not the kind of guy to pressure me. Sure, we were both tempted, but he led our dating relationship in a godly manner. The temptation I struggled with and against came from lies I believed about my worth and old wounds in my soul that the Enemy targeted inside me.

Living in a rom-com world doesn't make it easy for a woman to value sexual purity. TV programs and Hollywood films celebrate casual sex and mock those who value purity. At every turn we are confronted with sexual images, and we're brainwashed to believe that sex outside of marriage is the norm and that a woman's worth is found in being sexually desirable by a man. This redefining of a woman's value and the normalizing of promiscuity influences a Christian woman's thinking and, therefore, her behavior.

Our culture is hostile to God's design for sex and opposes those who stand for it. For example, a recent popular movie depicts the leading man saying that sex, now called a hookup, is just like "playing tennis." It's just physical. It's "no big deal." For a woman living in this culture that opposes God's highest and best, standing against these worldly influences becomes extremely difficult when romantic love has blurred your radar for Enemy fire. It's easy to shrug and say, "Everyone's doing it."

Purity, born out of love for Jesus, proved to be a war fought on three battlegrounds: a world-system opposed to God, an ancient foe who hates God and His glory, and my own ugly sinful nature. While my heart longed to live for God's glory and experience His highest and best, I was a girl living in Enemy-occupied territory. The war raged both around me and within me. Although my heart wanted to honor Jesus with sexual purity, I've never experienced a greater struggle with temptation in my entire life.

Thankfully, a moment of clarity in the midst of infatuation enabled me to look down to see a little red light blinking on my chest and realize that I was positioned squarely in the Enemy's cross hairs. He not only wanted me to fall into sin, but he especially wanted to sow seeds of destruction that would bear bitter fruit in my marriage and detour me away from God's highest and best. Satan, the Father of Lies, is brilliant at making sin look delicious while downplaying the deadly consequences.

Thankfully, I can praise God and say by His power and grace that Satan didn't win. Sure, we struggled, but we chose to stand our ground, we chose to resist the Enemy, we chose to say no to our fleshly desires, and we chose to fight for purity. Yes, Jesus was victorious, but I experienced just enough of Satan's schemes to know that this war is absolutely intense. But I also know, as a woman on the other side of marriage, that our choice to fight was more than worth it. God's best was worth fighting for, worth waiting for, and worth praying for.

The War Against the Soul

History is filled with tales of battles that turned the tide of war. The tide turned for me while reading Scripture during my quiet time with the Lord. Weak and desperate for help, I turned to God's Word for strength and guidance and landed on a verse that exploded like a truth grenade in my heart and mind. First Peter 2:11 says, "Abstain from fleshly lusts, which wage war against the soul" (KJV). I'd probably read that passage a hundred times before, but that day the words jumped off the page. The Lord wanted me to see the bigger picture—the war over sex.

The passage is a message to Christ-followers, men and women who love God yet live in the midst of a culture opposed to Christ. Sound familiar? The apostle Peter writes, "You are a chosen people, a royal priesthood, a holy nation, God's special possession, that you may declare the praises of him who called you out of darkness into his wonderful light. Once you were not a people, but now you are the people of God; once you had not received mercy, but now you have received mercy" (1 Peter 2:9–10). As I studied this passage, I realized the primary purpose of the text was to remind Christians of our true identity in Christ. It is for sons and daughters of the Most High God to remember that we are holy, children of God. In the midst of a godless world, we may feel like an alien, but we must remember that this world is not our home. As cherished daughters of God, we should not conform to this world.

Grasping this revelation prepared me for the truth that landed next. Because of our identity in Christ, we must "abstain from fleshly lusts, which wage war against the soul."

The word *abstain* means "to refrain, withdraw, or go without." This word calls us to live differently from those around us who indulge in sexual sin and who dismiss God's commandments. As cherished women, we choose to abstain because we know who we are—*holy*—but we also choose to abstain because we recognize that these "fleshly lusts wage war" against our souls.

Reading this text, I stopped and pondered two words. *"Wage war." . . . Wage war? Did the Bible actually just say that? OH! Wage WAR!*

Scenes from war movies began scrolling through my mind. I envisioned a great battle with opposing forces fighting to gain ground. As the Scripture came alive, the truth resonated in my heart—this was a war for my soul!

God's Word opened my eyes to see that the temptations, the lies, the fears, the media onslaught—the enormous battle raging around me and within me—was all concentrated on one thing: *a war for my soul!*

This revelation opened my eyes to see that my personal struggle with temptation was a far greater issue than I first recognized.

Sure, there are ample consequences to sex outside of God's design, but there proves a bigger story unfolding here. This battle is bigger than purity rings. Souls are at stake. And the Enemy knows this full well. For this reason, he unleashes hell's arsenals. The sexualization of our culture—the brainwashing of a generation to think that sex is "no big deal" and the onslaught of lies aimed at a woman's identity—are ultimately weapons in Satan's great war for souls.

With my newfound revelation came fresh resolve. I did not want the Enemy to win! He had stolen too many years in my past—years that I did not walk with Jesus—and I did not want to give him one more day of my life to rule and reign. Those days were over. Resolved to fight, I sought to learn more about the realities of spiritual warfare.

Clouds parting, the truth began to dawn on me. This battle is bigger than me. It's bigger than my story. This war against sexual purity is for my soul and ultimately God's glory, and I am not the only one in this fight. A generation of God's daughters—cherished ones—are buying in to the Enemy's lies. Sadly, many are deceived and living painfully defeated lives.

> For our struggle is not against flesh and blood, but against the rulers, against the powers, against the world forces of this darkness, against spiritual forces of wickedness in the heavenly places.
>
> Ephesians 6:12 NASB

It was a million tiny little things that, when you added them all up, they meant we were supposed to be together . . . and I knew it.

~ Sam Baldwin (Tom Hanks)
in *Sleepless in Seattle*

4

Good Intentions Aren't Good Enough

Eighty percent of young, unmarried Christians have had sex. Two-thirds have been sexually active in the last year. Even though, according to a recent Gallup poll, 76 percent of evangelicals believe sex outside of marriage is morally wrong.

—*Relevant*, August 2011

I first noticed her from the corner of my eye as I answered questions and signed books. She waited off to the side. I glanced up every now and then, and she still waited. This young woman waited until everyone else was gone. She had something she needed to talk to me about, but she wanted to do it in private. She waited for all of her friends and peers to leave. Turns out she had something to confess. She desperately needed to tell someone what she had done. Was still doing. And her shame and bewilderment overwhelmed her.

She looked as pure as the driven snow, as they say. In fact, she looked just like Snow White. Her story is a common one for a Christian girl her age. Her parents are still married. They are God-fearing, God-teaching parents. They did everything they knew to be right in raising her. She attended Sunday school, youth group, and Christian camps in the summer. She had a great relationship with her father. In fact, he escorted her to her purity ball. Her story didn't give the typical warning signs of looming bad choices. She attended church regularly and dated only fellow believers.

All the while, outside her parents' shield of safety and purity, a battle was brewing. While she lived at home, the battle seemed far away—a war on different soil, involving different people. Not her people. She was known as a "good girl" from a good family, with good support, good biblical teaching, and a good young man for a boyfriend. If you had asked her in high school if she intended to remain a virgin until she married, she would have answered with both passion and conviction, "Yes!"

And then she went to college.

The irony hit me like a tsunami, as she stood wiping away the torrents of tears falling from her eyes with the very hand on which her "purity ring" was prominently displayed. She had never seen the Enemy assault coming. Within weeks of living on a college campus, far from the bubble of protection in which she had grown so comfortable and so complacent, she fell on the battlefield that she didn't even know existed. And in the blink of an eye the wait was over. And so was her commitment to sexual purity.

Guilt, shame, and fear engulfed this battle-assaulted young woman. She is now wounded. She is bloodied by the flyby of the Enemy fire that caught her off guard and ill prepared. She had the knowledge. She had the support. She had the will. So what happened? Why did she lose the very first round?

I believe she was not prepared to face the battle. And . . . she was "in love." She hoped they would get married. She was afraid to lose him. And so the story goes. Her purity ring did not protect her from the lies and the insecurities. For all of the talk and ceremony of purity, she was not aware of the ugliness and the covert tactics waged by a truly evil Enemy. When facing waves of temptation, she finally succumbed to the lie that said, "Everyone is doing it." She slipped her purity ring off and placed it on his bedside table.

Spiritual Warfare

We are in battle—a battle far more fierce and strategic than any Alexander, Hannibal, or Napoleon ever fought. We must realize that no one prepares for a battle of which he is unaware, and no ones wins a battle for which he doesn't prepare.[1]

—T. C. Muck

The previous story is a true account of a young woman on the frontline in the war against sexual purity. But I've met hundreds of women who match her description. As I've traveled the country speaking at events, I meet women who know and love Jesus yet feel like they are trapped in Satan's prison. They listen as I share the Gospel and God's glorious design for sex within the covenant of marriage. Then, after the talk, they find me and through tears ask, "How did I get here? Marian, I am a Christian. I knew better. I knew I should've waited, but I didn't."

Broken. Confused. Women of all ages are lured into sexual sin, and once there, they feel trapped. They don't know how to break free and are too ashamed to bring their shame into the Light. Many times their souls are bonded to the man with whom they are involved and they have no idea how to stop or to break the soul tie that formed. They don't know how to fight the Enemy they now realize is so very real.

What is at stake in this war is a bigger deal than keeping a pledge made at a purity ring ceremony. We must understand that a full-scale spiritual war rages around and within women. The battles we face prove varied and numerous, but the war is both spiritual and physical in nature, both global and personal in location, and both ancient and present in its timing. I should know. I've experienced this war on many different battlefields.

I've told you about my history of hookups and heartbreaks, but what I failed to mention is that I, too, "knew better." It's hard for me to share my testimony because I am one of those women who has trouble pinpointing precisely when my relationship with God began. I grew up in a Christian home with Christian values. I knew sex was designed for marriage. Growing up, I believed the facts pertaining to Christianity, but I didn't know Jesus as my Lord and Savior. I knew rules and religion, and from both of these I rebelled. By the time my teenage years rolled around, I embraced the values of the world and threw myself into the college party scene. I fell into sexual sin and was sucked into a vortex of darkness. Satan's lies kept me locked like a prisoner of war in a cell of shame and regret. I experienced freedom only when Jesus redeemed me.

Today, I understand Satan's schemes from both perspectives: as the teenage girl who knew the "rules" but didn't have a love relationship with Jesus, and as a woman who loves Jesus with her whole heart yet has battled temptation. I know firsthand that our Enemy sets his cross hairs on God's girls—of all ages—and there is definitely a war against our souls.

Jesus said, "You will know the truth, and the truth will set you free" (John 8:32). God's Word set me free from the snares of Satan, and I can't hold back from sharing this freedom with others. Spiritual warfare is a reality, but I can't just hide in a foxhole while my sisters in Christ remain in bondage. I can't keep silent, I must speak up.

Stu Weber once said, "Every Christian is a walking battlefield."[2] Whether we like it or not, we are in a fight. Scripture teaches the realities of our fight on the three battlegrounds: the world, the flesh, and the devil. The worldly and demonic systems are external to us as believers, but they entice and provide opportunities for our flesh, which is the capacity for sin within us.

In this war, it is our own natural desires that are utilized by the Enemy to defeat us. A woman's longing for love and acceptance is the bull's-eye upon which the Enemy fixes his gaze. Concerning this battle, Kenneth Boa writes:

> Why do so many believers continue to act as nonbelievers when it comes to the quest for security, meaning and fulfillment in life? The answer lies in the fact that three powerful forces oppose our walking in the Spirit: the flesh, the world, and the devil (Ephesians 2:2–3). We live in a culture that promotes values and perspectives that are totally opposed to those of the Bible. Even though Scripture tells us that we are pilgrims and strangers on earth and that our citizenship is in heaven, we are prone to live as though this physical existence is the supreme reality. Unless we habitually reprogram our minds with the truth of Scripture, we will be profoundly influenced by culture. Satan and his minions utilize the world and the flesh to accomplish their purpose of defeating the lives of Christians and rendering them ineffective.[3]

For Christians, our battle with sexual sin is just one aspect of the greater war against Satan and his schemes to entice our flesh and conform us to the world.

You may be surprised to find the topic of spiritual warfare in a book about sexual purity. There is a reason. When I think of the Christian women who have fallen into sexual sin, I see two primary factors causing their defeat. First, they did not realize there was a war raging all around them. Second, most were either apathetic or naïve about our Enemy and his schemes.

Most of us don't like to think about spiritual warfare or the fact that we have an Enemy, but the Bible doesn't leave us that option. In Ephesians, Paul outlines for Christians the essentials of our faith: our salvation in Christ, our identity as God's children, and our common battle against unseen forces in the spiritual realm. Paul concludes this book with these words:

> Finally, be strong in the Lord and in his mighty power. Put on the full armor of God, so that you can take your stand against the devil's schemes. For our struggle is not against flesh and blood, but against the rulers, against the authorities, against the powers of this dark world and against the spiritual forces of evil in the heavenly realms. Therefore put on the full armor of God, so that when the day of evil comes, you may be able to stand your ground, and after you have done everything, to stand.
>
> Ephesians 6:10–13

Please note how clear and precise God's direction is to believers—Satan is real and we are at war. We are told to equip ourselves with armor—not "if" evil comes, but "when" it does.

Satan flat-out hates marriage. He despises a covenant built upon a vow to "love, honor, and cherish," because a biblical marriage is a picture of Christ's sacrificial love for His church. He especially hates God's glory—and love, sex, and marriage are all designed to perfectly reflect our glorious covenant relationship with God. John and Stasi Eldredge, in *Love and War*, echo this truth by saying, "The devil hates marriage; he hates the beautiful picture of Jesus and His Bride that it represents. He hates love and life and beauty in all its forms."[4] So Satan unleashed a full-fledged war against marriage. This war results in countless casualties: broken hearts, broken dreams, and broken promises. Satan begins his assault on a marriage covenant long before a girl even meets her future husband.

Ladies, before you get depressed with all this talk of warfare, let me offer this word of truth to give you hope: Satan doesn't determine your destiny. Jesus determines your destiny. Victory is attainable. We can stand in Christ and experience the abundant life He promises, but we must be equipped with God's truth, and we must deal with the areas in our lives that are open doors for Enemy attack. I wish I could sit with you right now, face-to-face, and tell you this next statement: It is never too late. Friend, it doesn't matter if you struggled yesterday or are battling temptation today, it is never too late to stand against the evil one and experience the blessings that follow obedience. Our God is a great Redeemer, and He specializes in restoration. Keep reading. Keep standing. Keep trusting.

I've had the joy of ministering to women from all walks of life. I've met women who do not know the Lord, who are enslaved to darkness, yet upon hearing the Gospel experience freedom and life in a relationship with Jesus Christ. These women are gloriously set free! I've also met women who were raised in the church, who know Jesus, yet at some point turned away from Him. These women turned from their freedom to bondage. As I minister to the second group, these women are returning to Christ in repentance. Let me make this point clear: It doesn't matter if you are new to the Christian faith or if you are a woman who walked away. Either way, God is able to redeem your story for His glory.

Both groups of women must know that our destiny is not determined by past choices but by our great God. God is able to deliver both the woman who was captive to darkness for years and the girl who knew better. But Satan will not let go without a fight. It is often said that while he can't take away our salvation, he would love to take away our destinies. He knows God offers abundant life to His children who follow Him in obedience. Satan hates this and does not want you glorifying God or experiencing His best in your life. For this reason, spiritual warfare is a reality we all face.

Though we live in the world, we do not wage war as the world does. The weapons we fight with are not the weapons of the world. On the contrary, they have divine power to demolish strongholds.

We demolish arguments and every pretension that sets itself up against the knowledge of God, and we take captive every thought to make it obedient to Christ.

2 Corinthians 10:3–5

There is a third group of women I want to address—the ones who have waited. The ones who are seeking to honor God with their purity. This book is also for you—to encourage you in your wait and to equip you for the day of temptation. One thing Scripture tells us with certainty is that we all experience times of temptation and will face seasons of attack when we must stand against the Enemy. It's easy to think we are immune to the lures and lies, but that thinking proves to be one of Satan's best weapons—pride. Like a lion seeking prey, our Enemy knows that when our defenses are down and when we are deluded into thinking we are beyond falling, we are the most vulnerable.

Yes, dear ones, we are at war, but we aren't victims. This book is written to both equip you for victory and to encourage you to wait for God's highest and best. Armed with God's Word, the sword of the Spirit, I feel called to be part of a holy resistance . . . *the resistance of the cherished ones.* We are daughters of the Most High God who understand our identity in Christ; we refuse to settle for the Enemy's schemes and, in the midst of a world opposed to God, choose to fight for, wait for, and pray for God's highest and best.

Arise, cherished ones!

You have bewitched me, body and soul,
and *I love, I love, I love you.*

~ Mr. Darcy (Matthew Macfadyen)
in *Pride & Prejudice*

5

Vision

Marriage is the sanctuary God created for sex, and only there in the refuge of covenantal love, will you find sex at its best.

—John and Stasi Eldredge, *Love and War*

Vision vs. Rules

In a culture where microwaves are considered slow, movies are on demand, and a five-minute wait at a fast-food restaurant requires a tremendous amount of patience, we tend to expect immediate gratification at every turn. I know I'm not immune to this cultural expectation. Our world lives in the "now." For most of us, putting off desires until the future goes against every fiber of our being. How, then, does our generation choose to wait for sex until marriage in an "on demand" world?

Proverbs 29:18 says, "Where there is no vision, the people are unrestrained, but happy is he who keeps the law" (NASB). Another version translates the passage this way: "Without prophetic vision people run wild" (GW). Could it be that many Christian women "go wild" because they simply lack vision for God's glorious plan for sex and marriage? Sexual purity requires more than just rules—women today need to envision the beauty of God's design and know why purity is *worth fighting for.*

My great hope in writing is not to pen yet another book about Christian dating. Will we discuss dating? Yes, of course, but dating isn't our objective. While I'm at it, this also isn't just another book on sexual purity. Frankly, there are many fine resources available. Will we discover biblical strategies for sexual purity? Absolutely! Beyond these two fine agendas, there is a greater purpose that propels me to write.

I feel called to impart truth to a generation entangled in lies from the Enemy. I want to equip my sisters in Christ to fight for God's highest and best. I hurt for women who dream of being cherished yet believe Satan's lies that take them away from their hearts' true desire. My heart breaks for women who long to be treasured yet settle for so much less. I should know; I was once that girl.

I get it. In the moment of temptation, it is hard to remember *why* you are resisting unless your heart is fully convinced that saying no to temptation today is actually saying yes to a better blessing tomorrow. Unless a woman understands *why* she is fighting, then she will not be equipped to stand against the onslaught of lies and temptations specifically designed to seduce her into sexual sin. When purity proves difficult, a woman who lacks vision will eventually wave the white flag of surrender. As we know, simply wearing a purity ring doesn't guarantee victory. A Christian woman needs a God-sized *vision* of why she is waiting.

Yes, I said "vision."

Vision: the ability to think about and plan for the future, using intelligence and imagination, someone's idea or hope of how something should be done, or how it will be in the future. A mental image produced by the imagination.[1]

Why is vision essential to winning the battle for sexual purity? Because of this truth: Rules will be broken, but visions are lived. If a woman fixes her eye on the prize, she will make life choices that align with her vision. Allow me to illustrate.

Imagine someone establishes a "rule" that says I must wake up every morning at five to run ten miles. Two problems: (1) I'm not much of a morning person, and (2) I'm more likely to run ten miles if being chased by an armed gunman. So when I'm presented with the "rule," the questions and excuses start flying: "Why should I?" "Why ten miles?" "What if I don't like running?" "But I'm more of a Pilates girl!" After the initial complaints are thrown about, I begrudgingly decide to obey, but of course I don't really want to.

What do you suppose would happen the next morning? More questions and complaints would probably start firing: "Do I want to get out of bed? No! Sleep = good. Run = bad!" More than likely I would want to hit Snooze and snuggle back under the blanket.

Let's just imagine that I tumbled out of bed and hit the track. Now picture me there, on the track, in a cute little running outfit (of course), and stretching out for my ten-mile run. Off I would go. Running . . . running . . . running . . . (I'm such a liar. At an eleven-minute-mile pace, I couldn't honestly call myself a runner. I'm more of what you'd call a very slow jogger.) Halfway through mile number four I would desperately want to quit. Why? Because it wouldn't feel good! At the first sign of discomfort, my flesh would want to break the "rule" and do what my body would scream at me to do, which is to *immediately stop running*.

Right about the time that my flesh would start to beg for a donut shop, those seductive voices would begin to whisper. (You know the ones that just love to justify breaking rules.) Eventually, I would probably cave in to the voices. The primary problem would not be my lack of athletic prowess or the fact that I don't like early mornings. The issue would be that I didn't have a passion for running. I was only running to follow a rule, which didn't offer much of a compelling reason to overcome the obstacles.

Rules will be broken, but visions are lived.

Now consider this scenario. Today, as I write, the world's eyes are fixed on the Summer Olympic Games. This is prime-time, world-class, top-notch competition at its finest. Athletes from across the globe have envisioned this moment all of their lives. The goal of competing in the Olympic games was the vehicle that drove years of disciplined training. Why does this matter? Vision proves a powerful motivator.

Imagine a young woman who dreamed of competing in the Olympics her whole life. As a little girl she watched athletes from her country step onto the medal platform to receive gold while their national anthems played. She wept with every victory and thought, *One day that will be me,* every day envisioning the day when she, too, would compete.

As she grew up, running wasn't a "rule" but a way of life. To achieve her goal, she trained. The more she ran, the more she loved the sport. Her vision shaped her life choices. She was propelled to live a disciplined life, not in order to keep a rule but because of her great passion for the prize. Was she tired some days and dreaded the early morning wake-up calls? Of course, but she kept training. Each day that she ran was one step closer to her goal—Olympic gold.

What's the difference between my example of running to obey a rule and the Olympic athlete? *Vision.* This truth is a game changer in our battle for sexual purity. Vision enables us to make choices along the way to overcome temptations to quit, to persevere when facing challenges, and to say no to temporary pleasures in order to say yes to our dreams. Why? *Rules will be broken, but visions are lived.*

The same principle holds true for the single Christian woman who desires God's highest and best. Sexual purity is not about following a set of rules; it is about vision. I've read so many books about sex for Christian women. Most of them have a chapter that addresses the big question: *How far is too far?* While this is a perfectly valid question, I think we must first start with the big picture and answer the question of *why*. Instead of asking *How far is too far?* we must be women of vision who understand *why* purity is worth fighting for.

When you know that you are cherished and understand who you are in Christ, then you don't want to settle for anything less than God's beautiful design for sex within marriage. My desire is to impart a vision that you will choose to live for instead of a rule that you will choose to break. For the woman who longs to be cherished, she must have a vision for sexual purity that carries her through the battles she will inevitably face along the way.

A Woman of Vision Grasps the Heart of Obedience

When I married Justin, not only did God bless me with an amazing man to call my husband, but I also became a stepmom to two incredible little boys. I adore these guys so much and call them my "bonus boys." The transition from single girl to Mom happened for me overnight. It's been a whirlwind of change. Honestly, I never imagined myself in this role, but these two young men truly are God's surprise "bonus" to my life.

After we married, we bought a house together for our new family. Our home has stairs with slick hardwood floors. We quickly realized that running on the stairs would be dangerous for the boys, so we sat them down and told them, "No running on the stairs." For two little boys under the age of ten, running is second nature. Therefore, we explained *why* they couldn't run on the stairs. As their dad and stepmom, we could foresee dangers that they could not. We knew the potential of a big fall and an injured little boy. We said, "Trust us, this is for your own good." We repeated the instructions several times over a few days, and eventually everyone complied by carefully walking down the stairs.

Have you ever heard the expression "Some lessons are learned the hard way"? I recently learned "the hard way" the heart of obedience. A few weeks later, the boys and I were upstairs when the doorbell rang. I'd been waiting for a delivery, so I jumped up and sprinted down the stairs. When my foot hit the landing between the two stories, I slipped and my body propelled forward into the air, landing me face first on the hard, cold ground ten steps below.

Dazed and confused, pain ripped through my body. I looked up to see the boys standing above me, wagging their heads and saying, "You aren't supposed to run down the stairs." Yep, I learned the hard way.

It took a few minutes to gather myself. My arm began to swell with black-and-blue bruises and became almost impossible to move. My body ached all over from hitting the stone tile. I was beat up but otherwise okay. It could have been so much worse. As I pulled myself together, it was now painfully clear why we set a house rule for no running on the stairs. The rule wasn't to keep us from having fun; the heart behind the rule was loving protection.

The same holds true for God's commandments concerning sex. God is our heavenly Father, and just as any good parent desires to protect his or her child, He wants to protect us. He designed us body, soul, and spirit, and He also created sex. As our Creator, God knows better than anyone the consequences of sex outside of a covenant. He knows the long-term implications and ramifications of sexual intimacy outside of marriage. He knows the dangers and seeks to protect us from harm and heartbreak.

For the single Christian woman, sexual purity is more than just following a rule; it is about living for a vision. Sure, God gives us commandments, but we must understand that the "rule" comes from the heart of God, who loves us more than we love ourselves. God desires to protect us. Therefore, He establishes boundaries for our own good. Once we grasp this truth, our desires change. We recognize that our heavenly Father isn't keeping us from pleasure; He seeks to preserve us so that we can experience His highest and best.

A Woman of Vision Understands God's Design for Sex

While we live in a romantic-comedy world, which depicts sex as merely a recreational activity, God's message is that sex is a profound mystery, a glorious union between a man and a woman where two become one. The Bible says:

> There's more to sex than mere skin on skin. Sex is as much spiritual mystery as physical fact. As written in Scripture, "The two become one." . . . We must not pursue the kind of sex that avoids commitment and intimacy, leaving us more lonely than ever—the kind of sex that can never "become one." There is a sense in which sexual sins are different from all others. In sexual sin we violate the sacredness of our own bodies, these bodies that were made for God-given and God-modeled love, for "becoming one" with another.
>
> 1 Corinthians 6:16–18 THE MESSAGE

Stop. Think. Marvel. "The two become one." I hate to be the one to break the news to Hollywood, but sex isn't "just like tennis." It is a really big deal. A profound mystery. Move over, *Cosmopolitan*, no one knows more about sex than God does. (Feel free to fire all of your so-called "experts.") Because . . . *wait for it* . . .
God
Invented
Sex.
He, better than anyone, knows how we can experience the best. He also knows the dangers we face when we ignore His design.

One Flesh

Sex is a blending of souls and is not to be tampered with in an unholy fashion. Sex was created to bond a man and woman together . . . *for life.* In the Bible, we are told that in marriage a man leaves his father and his mother, "and shall cleave unto his wife: and they shall be one flesh" (Genesis 2:24 KJV). To become "one flesh" implies the union of man and woman in a sexual relationship. In the original language of this verse, the word for *cleave* is the same word for *glue.*

Often you'll hear people naïvely say that marriage is "just a piece of paper." This notion is so far from the truth. A contract is written on a piece of paper; a covenant is written on hearts. There is a vast difference between the two. In a contract, people are looking out for themselves and asking, "What's in this for me?" In the marriage covenant, however, a man and a woman stand at an altar, before God, and promise to lay their lives down for one another.

In biblical times, covenants were sealed by blood. The marriage covenant is sealed by the physical act of sex, with the giving of bodies and souls to one another. Sex is the consummation of the covenant. But that's not all. Sex was created to cleave together the husband and wife. *Cleave?* Now, that's a straight-up Bible word if there ever was one. But this word is so filled with truth that we need to take time to unpack it so we know why we are waiting.

God designed sex to be a bonding mechanism, or the superglue, between the husband and wife, by which they become *one.* When two people have sex, not only do bodies join, but their souls unite and they bond to one another in a mysterious way. This bonding works beautifully within the context of marriage. But outside of marriage, this bonding can cause emotional heartache and deep and lasting damage to the soul.

Sadly, our world has made common what God made sacred. And the aftermath of this brainwashing has left a generation facing heartbreak, disease, unplanned pregnancy, uncommitted relationships, prolonged singleness, not to mention shame and regret. Sex outside of God's design has devastating emotional and physical consequences. Despite what our favorite television shows and movies portray, there are real-life consequences that real women face, and they don't easily resolve at the end of a thirty-minute program. These issues, for many women, are life-changing.

Our "no strings attached" culture likes to promote the idea that condoms are the key to safe sex. Believing this lie has led to unspeakable emotional and physical harm. We must wake up and see that we are more than just physical bodies; we are souls that are affected by what we do with our bodies. Sex is not just physical; it is spiritual. As *The Message* says so beautifully in 1 Corinthians 6:16–18, "There's more to sex than mere skin on skin. Sex is as much spiritual mystery as physical fact." While the bruises from a fall down the stairs may last a few weeks and fade away, the bruises to a soul can last a lifetime.

> Flee from sexual immorality. All other sins a person commits are outside the body, but whoever sins sexually, sins against their own body.
>
> 1 Corinthians 6:18

Soul Ties

God is so smart! His extraordinary design is brilliant! His glorious creative power is on display in how perfectly He designed sex to bond a couple within the covenant of marriage. In her book *Sex and the Soul of a Woman*, Paula Rinehart writes:

> God knew it would take something special between a man and a woman to bear the weight of life together. Bonding means that

when you are irritated with your man, when you hate his haircut—even when he does something terribly disappointing—you are still deeply connected.[2]

God wired us to bond through sexual intimacy. This is a physical reality as well as a spiritual one. During sex, hormones are released in both the male and female. In the woman, a powerful hormone called oxytocin is released; this hormone is what causes women to emotionally bond and glue to the man. The more oxytocin is released, the more bonding ensues. Researchers know that oxytocin is produced naturally in the brain and that it is released when a couple becomes physically intimate, most especially during sexual orgasm, producing strong bonding in both men and women. For women, it increases trust and immediately produces feelings of attachment.[3] This attachment is both physical and spiritual and is called a "soul tie." Soul ties occur regardless of whether people are married. Hence the devastation a woman feels when the breakup occurs.

There is also a powerful hormone released in men during sex called vasopressin. Vasopressin is often called the "monogamy gene." This hormone is what causes a man to feel protective toward and want to provide for the woman with whom he is having sex. But when a man and woman engage in sex outside of marriage, these hormones designed by God to create a strong, lasting marriage actually begin to work against the couple. This backfire causes mistrust, insecurity, and abandonment.[4]

Without the assurance of the covenant, a woman's soul feels jeopardized and she does not feel cherished. In the romantic comedy *He's Just Not That Into You*, starring Jennifer Aniston, her character faces this exact situation. She is living with a man who will not marry her. Their relationship is sexual. On one hand, she tries to convince herself that she is happy with the arrangement, but as the movie unfolds, we see her soul craves more. She can't continue on without the security of the covenant—it's just how a woman is wired. There is truly something supernatural about a covenant, and when it precedes sexual intimacy, a woman feels security and freedom.

As a side note, when I refer to sexual intimacy, I'm including all types of sexual expressions, not just intercourse. A common misconception among Christians is that "everything but" intercourse is fair game. It is my belief that the biblical understanding of the word *sex* is meant to include all intimate acts: foreplay, oral sex, touching, etc. Oxytocin is released through intimate touch and arousal, not just during intercourse. Many Christian women operate on the terms of "technical virginity" although they are practicing sexual acts with their boyfriends.

Oxytocin causes a woman to cling to the man she is physically involved with, while vasopressin causes a man to feel the necessity of commitment. If he is not obligated to her (i.e., through marriage), the hormone causes him to "freak out" and pull back from the relationship.[5]

In marriage, the attachment created by the sexual bond is designed to help a couple stay connected and deal with the natural difficulties and human flaws that inevitably arise from living with another person (e.g., loving a guy who leaves the toilet seat up, who gains twenty pounds, and who forgets your birthday). But forming such a sexual attachment in an unmarried relationship leads to several significant risks:

- When a relationship between a man and a woman ends and the sexual bond is broken, intense emotional pain occurs.
- The forming and breaking of sexual bonds through casual sex or multiple long-term sexual partners lessens a person's ability to bond rightly in future relationships.
- When a woman bonds sexually to a man, she often mistakes this bond for real love and could marry the wrong person. Sex literally masks the true problems in a relationship.

- Women often find themselves "stuck" in an unhealthy relationship because their hearts are superglued to a guy who isn't good for them. We've all seen a girl—or perhaps you are that girl—caught in an unhealthy relationship that she can't leave because she "loves" him. Or a couple that knows they are not right for each other may break up, only to get back together and break up again repeatedly. What keeps them returning to the scene of the crime? *Often* it is the pull of the sexual attachment.[6]

A soul tie is far more than a physical reality that fades once the relationship is over. A soul tie is just as the name describes—a connection between two souls as a result of sex. As Erwin Lutzer explains in his book *Putting Your Past Behind You*:

> Sex creates a "soul tie" between two people, forming the most intimate of all human relationships. When the Bible says, "Adam knew Eve his wife" (Genesis 4:1 KJV), the word *know* is not simply a euphemism for the sex act. Sexual intercourse actually consummates the highest form of human interpersonal communication and knowledge. Indeed, this exclusive familiarity cannot be easily erased. Once a man and a woman have had sex together, nothing can be the same between them ever again.[7]

Here's the thing: We can't unwire the way God wired us. Just as gravity is a law of nature and works as God designed it, so does sex.

Have you noticed the plethora of films that revolve around the "friends with benefits" plot? There are several with this theme. The movie typically starts with two people attempting to have a sexual relationship that doesn't include feelings or any type of emotional connection (aka strings). They call these *romantic comedies* because the notion is just laughable. (Insert eye roll.)

Lo and behold, every one of these movies ends with the same conclusion—the two people couldn't keep their commitment to "no strings attached." Why? Because our bodies are wired to bond. It's just that simple. Yet over and over again media tries to shove down our throats this garbage that what we do with our bodies doesn't affect our souls. (Please forgive the passion. I just get a little worked up when I see the lies that bombard women and lead them down a path of destruction.)

I realize most Christian women aren't tempted by the hookup culture that is so normalized in our society. Most Christian women do have higher standards than the world, because we do actually desire "strings." Our struggle emerges when we are "in love" with the one that we ~~think~~ hope is "the one." It is at this point that sex outside of marriage seems justifiable.

Christian women struggle with temptation most when in committed relationships that they hope will progress to marriage. Ask any woman who has walked through a painful breakup and she will tell you that she thought she was in love with "the one." The sad reality is, most of these relationships end long before they end up at the altar. Ironically, it is actually the introduction of sex into the relationship that dooms it to destruction. (Satan is such a liar. He lures us with lies and then leaves us in a big fat mess.) The only way to truly guard your heart and protect your soul from damage is to choose to wait, not just until you are "in love," but until you say "I do."

After the breakup, many girls are left feeling empty, lonely, and worthless. These emotions can result in a vicious cycle. Once the insecurity takes over, girls often resort to new sexual encounters to combat the emptiness and loneliness they now feel. Many women try to convince themselves that they just don't care. Others build huge walls of defense to protect themselves against the emotional pain. These defensive walls keep them from experiencing the true love and intimacy they desire. Regardless of the response, none of this emotional destruction is God's will for women. God's design for sex is for our good, and when we follow His guidelines, we don't reap this kind of emotional turmoil.

Worth Waiting For

In our culture, women face strong opposing messages when it comes to sex. On one hand, we get the message that "Sex is just sex; it's no big deal." Hopefully by now we understand that sex is a *really* big deal. When we buy this lie and tell ourselves, "I shouldn't care that he won't commit or that he has moved on to another girl," we settle for so much less than God's best.

You are worth much more than that kind of treatment. Recall what 1 Corinthians 6 says: "In sexual sin we violate the sacredness of our own bodies" (v. 16–20 THE MESSAGE). Your body is sacred, holy ground. Therefore, you have every right to care! Your heavenly Father created you for something much more glorious.

On the other hand, we are bombarded with another dangerous message: A woman's worth is found in being desired sexually by a man. Many women build their self-esteem on being an object of sexual desire. They think it is a compliment if a man wants to use them for sex. We've been brainwashed by media to see this kind of treatment as a good thing. It's gotten to the point that some actually believe it is flattering to be objectified. Gone are the days when women respected themselves enough to get angry when treated like an object. Today we not only expect it, but many actually like it. What message are we sending if we allow ourselves to be treated as a *something* instead of a *someone*? We are saying, "It's okay to use me. I'm just an object."

> Do you not know that your bodies are temples of the Holy Spirit, who is in you, whom you have received from God? You are not your own; you were bought at a price. Therefore honor God with your bodies.
>
> 1 Corinthians 6:19–20

Never forget, oh, cherished one, you belong to Jesus. You aren't an object. Think about that word, *object*. An object is something that is used. Is that really what you want? Do you want to be something that is simply used for someone else's pleasure? Or do you want more? I think we all, deep in our hearts, long to be cherished. I think most women want much more. And guess what? God wants more for you, too.

You are cherished.

You are a priceless treasure.

You are worth fighting for.

You are worth waiting for.

Do you hear these words? Better yet, do you believe these words? A woman of vision will believe one fundamental truth about herself: that she is, in fact, cherished. And, ladies, the man who cherishes you will wait for you.

Let us always keep in mind as we fight this fight that God's view of sex is so grand that He has one basic command: Any man who is worthy of having sex with you should be willing to die for you. *Die for me?* I know that sounds extreme, in a world where people have sex without even knowing each other's last names. Sex was created for the lifelong commitment of marriage. According to the Bible, in marriage the husband is to love his wife as Christ loves the church. Jesus gave His life up for you and me, and this sacrificial love is the model God gives for men in a marriage. Sacrificial, selfless, put-your-wife's-needs-first kind of love—that is God's best for you. That is a far cry from being an object.

So, ladies, my question is this: Why would we ever settle for anything less than God's best? God wants for you to be with a man who will not only be there in the morning but will also be there *every* morning . . . till death do you part. God wants for you to be with someone who will love you, not use you. You give up so much when you give in. You give away your own worth. You give away your mystery. You give away your soul. God wants so much more for you. Why? Because, my friend, *you* are cherished.

A Woman of Vision Stands

There are three characters in the Bible who absolutely captivate my attention because they were men of vision who chose to stand when everyone else bowed down to a false god. Their names are Shadrach, Meshach, and Abednego. These Hebrew young men lived as exiles in Babylon after the fall of Jerusalem. In 605 BC, Nebuchadnezzar, king of Babylon, conquered Judah (Daniel 1:1–2). Following his victory, Nebuchadnezzar ordered that the brightest young men of Judah be deported to Babylon. His plan was to train these young men for three years and then give some of them positions in the royal court (Daniel 1:3–5). Shadrach, Meshach, and Abednego were among this group.

The three years of training in Babylon were really an attempt to brainwash the Jewish captives. Nebuchadnezzar wanted Shadrach, Meshach, Abednego, and the others to become so indoctrinated in Babylonian culture that at the end of their training they would think and act like Babylonians. Even the names of the young men were changed. Shadrach, Meshach, and Abednego's original names were Hananiah, Mishael, and Azariah (Daniel 1:6–7). *Hananiah* means "Beloved of the Lord"; *Mishael* means "Who is as God"; and *Azariah* means "The Lord is my help." Their Jewish names honored the Lord, but their new names honored the gods of the Babylonians.[8]

Despite the constant pressure to conform to a godless culture, these three men loved and revered God. What especially impresses me is how they expressed their love for God under extreme pressure. They proved their love for God, not with words or with songs of worship, but with pure, undefiled obedience. The Babylonians could change their names, but they could not change their hearts. They would remain loyal to the God of Israel no matter what.

This is their story:

King Nebuchadnezzar built a gold statue, ninety feet high and nine feet thick. He set it up on the Dura plain in the province of Babylon. He then ordered all the important leaders in the province, everybody who was anybody, to the dedication ceremony of the statue. They all came for the dedication, all the important people, and took their places before the statue that Nebuchadnezzar had erected.

A herald then proclaimed in a loud voice: "Attention, everyone! Every race, color, and creed, listen! When you hear the band strike up—all the trumpets and trombones, the tubas and baritones, the drums and cymbals—fall to your knees and worship the gold statue that King Nebuchadnezzar has set up. Anyone who does not kneel and worship shall be thrown immediately into a roaring furnace."

The band started to play, a huge band equipped with all the musical instruments of Babylon, and everyone—every race, color, and creed—fell to their knees and worshiped the gold statue that King Nebuchadnezzar had set up.

Just then, some Babylonian fortunetellers stepped up and accused the Jews. They said to King Nebuchadnezzar, "Long live the king! You gave strict orders, O king, that when the big band started playing, everyone had to fall to their knees and worship the gold statue, and whoever did not go to their knees and worship it had to be pitched into a roaring furnace. Well, there are some Jews here—Shadrach, Meshach, and Abednego—whom you have placed in high positions in the province of Babylon. These men are ignoring you, O king. They don't respect your gods and they won't worship the gold statue you set up."

Furious, King Nebuchadnezzar ordered Shadrach, Meshach, and Abednego to be brought in. When the men were brought in, Nebuchadnezzar asked, "Is it true, Shadrach, Meshach, and Abednego, that you don't respect my gods and refuse to worship the gold statue that I have set up? I'm giving you a second chance—but from now on, when the big band strikes up you must go to your knees and worship the statue I have made. If you don't worship it, you will be pitched into a roaring furnace, no questions asked. Who is the god who can rescue you from my power?"

Daniel 3:1–15 THE MESSAGE

A gauntlet was thrown down in Babylon. Shadrach, Meshach, and Abednego could either bow down to the image of King Nebuchadnezzar or face the fiery furnace. This is faith put to the ultimate test. In the moment, I am certain that falling down before the image seemed like "no big deal" and would quickly eliminate heaps of problems. But there was one problem: God's glory.

These young Hebrew men knew one thing: There is only one true God, and He said, "Thou shalt have no other gods before me" (Exodus 20:3 KJV). For them to bow, along with the rest of Babylon, would be to defy and to deny their God.

Friends, as Christ-followers today, we, too, are living in our own kind of Babylon. For we also bear the name of God; we are His. And yet we live in a world that wants to conform us to its ways. Sexual promiscuity is the norm for those who do not know God, but it is not for the cherished daughters of the King. Like Shadrach, Meshach, and Abednego, we are bombarded by the constant onslaught of media—image after image, scene after scene, line after line. The worldview imprints upon our minds and we begin to see the world's values as "normal" and "acceptable." Through this indoctrination, Christian women are tempted to adopt a radically different worldview from that of the Bible—a worldview that disregards God, a worldview that degrades women, a worldview that cheapens sex, and a worldview that enslaves us to sin.

But we have a choice. Scripture teaches us, "Do not conform to the pattern of this world, but be transformed by the renewing of your mind" (Romans 12:2). This is precisely what three brave Hebrew men did in Babylon thousands of years ago. They chose not to conform to the pattern of the world around them.

> Shadrach, Meshach, and Abednego replied to him, "King Ne-buchadnezzar, we do not need to defend ourselves before you in this matter. If we are thrown into the blazing furnace, the God we serve is able to deliver us from it, and he will deliver us from Your Majesty's hand. But even if he does not, we want you to know, Your Majesty, that we will not serve your gods or worship the image of gold you have set up."
>
> Daniel 3:16–18 NIV

I love the boldness of these men! Shadrach, Meshach, and Abednego refused to worship and bow down to the king's image. In doing so, they placed their destinies in the hands of God. Their boldness is the rally cry of the one who knows and believes God. These men knew that obedience would come with a price.

I can't mince words here and deny reality. There was a serious consequence to their decision not to bow before the image. When they chose not to conform, it enraged the king to such a boiling point of fury that he had them thrown into a fiery furnace. Friends, I'm not going to sugarcoat this one. Sex is one of the chief false gods of our culture. If you refuse to bow down to the world's idol of sexual promiscuity, you, too, could face backlash. As a woman of God, you may find yourself in times of testing that feel like a fiery furnace.

- You may be mocked for your values.
- You may feel like you don't fit in.
- You may feel alone in your convictions.
- You may severely limit your dating options.
- You may even have family members who think you are a freak because you choose celibacy.

- You might at times feel awkward when conversations turn to sexual escapades and you don't have a tantalizing story to offer.

Don't allow these pressures to buckle your knees. Stand! It may be tough, but here's the thing: In your fiery furnace, there is One who is with you! The Lord God Almighty stands for you and fights for you in the midst of your fire, and He alone determines your destiny. Here is a promise to stand on: God blesses our obedience!

Nebuchadnezzar, his face purple with anger, cut off Shadrach, Meshach, and Abednego. He ordered the furnace fired up seven times hotter than usual. He ordered some strong men from the army to tie them up, hands and feet, and throw them into the roaring furnace. Shadrach, Meshach, and Abednego, bound hand and foot, fully dressed from head to toe, were pitched into the roaring fire. Because the king was in such a hurry and the furnace was so hot, flames from the furnace killed the men who carried Shadrach, Meshach, and Abednego to it, while the fire raged around Shadrach, Meshach, and Abednego.

Suddenly King Nebuchadnezzar jumped up in alarm and said, "Didn't we throw three men, bound hand and foot, into the fire?" "That's right, O king," they said. "But look!" he said. "I see four men, walking around freely in the fire, completely unharmed! And the fourth man looks like a son of the gods!"

Nebuchadnezzar went to the door of the roaring furnace and called in, "Shadrach, Meshach, and Abednego, servants of the High God, come out here!" Shadrach, Meshach, and Abednego walked out of the fire.

All the important people, the government leaders and king's counselors, gathered around to examine them and discovered that the fire hadn't so much as touched the three men—not a hair singed, not a scorch mark on their clothes, not even the smell of fire on them!

Daniel 3:19–27 THE MESSAGE

Cherished one, I can promise you that your battle for sexual purity will not be an easy one. I can guarantee there will be times that you will feel pressure to bow down to the gods of this world. But choose to stand! Stand up for the glory of God, no matter what fears or pressures you may face. And when you do, I can promise you this: He will be with you! Just as King Nebuchadnezzar saw a fourth man in the midst of the fire, Jesus will be with you whatever you may face: loneliness, ridicule, rejection, etc. One of my favorite Scriptures says it best:

> If God is for us, who is against us? He who did not spare His own Son, but delivered Him over for us all, how will He not also with Him freely give us all things? . . . For I am convinced that neither death, nor life, nor angels, nor principalities, nor things present, nor things to come, nor powers, nor height, nor depth, nor any other created thing, will be able to separate us from the love of God, which is in Christ Jesus our Lord.
>
> Romans 8:31–32, 38–39 NASB

You are cherished! He is with you and will never leave you nor forsake you. And guess what? Even when your choice to fight for purity seems unpopular, the Bible says, "If God is for you, who can be against you?" Ladies, you have the God of the universe fighting for you. When you commit to stand for Him, He unleashes the blessings of heaven on your behalf.

There is a second beautiful promise revealed in the lives of these three brave young men. When you choose to stand for God, He is glorified in and through your circumstances! When Shadrach, Meshach, and Abednego found themselves in the fire, yes, God was with them, and the most powerful man in the world was forced to acknowledge the fact that there is only One True God—the God of three brave Hebrew young men who refused to bow down.

> Nebuchadnezzar said, "Blessed be the God of Shadrach, Meshach, and Abednego! He sent his angel and rescued his servants who

trusted in him! They ignored the king's orders and laid their bodies on the line rather than serve or worship any god but their own."

Daniel 3:28 THE MESSAGE

Here is an old saying that I've put to the test and found to be true: "God blesses obedience." God made a universe in which righteousness is always rewarded in the long run and unrighteousness is always punished.

I the LORD search the heart and examine the mind, to reward each person according to their conduct, according to what their deeds deserve.

Jeremiah 17:10

Does not he who weighs the heart perceive it? Does not he who guards your life know it? Will he not repay everyone according to what they have done?

Proverbs 24:12

Yes, as Christians we do face trials and we will encounter various battles along the way, but we can never forget that God loves to bless His children. When we choose to glorify God through sexual purity, we put ourselves in a position to receive the good things He desires to give us. Think on these words that were spoken to King Asa, who found himself in the midst of a tough battle.

For the eyes of the LORD move to and fro throughout the earth that He may strongly support those whose heart is completely His.

2 Chronicles 16:9 NASB

This word promises that God will strongly support those whose hearts belong to Him. Cherished ones, I can't promise you how or tell you when, but when you choose to stand for God, He will glorify himself in and through your life. I was single for a very, very, very long time. (I almost typed one more "very" just for emphasis, but I figured you get the point.) Those years were in many ways a fiery furnace in which my heart was tested in the crucible of waiting. Yet in the wait I experienced the sweet presence of Christ. He was always with me. The biggest blessing of obedience is Christ himself. As Psalm 16:11 says, "In Your presence is fullness of joy" (NASB). Whether we are married or single, He is the One our hearts hunger for, and when we choose to stand for Him, we experience more of Him.

Standing for sexual purity may seem ridiculous to the world, but when we do so, we place our destinies in the hands of the One who is the giver of every good and perfect gift. There were many times I felt the pressure to compromise on my standards and date guys who didn't share my love for Jesus or passion for purity, but if I had done so, I would have missed out on God's highest and best for my life. I can look back and see the undeniable hand of God's faithfulness. My refusal to compromise enabled the Lord to glorify His name by providing the desire of my heart for a husband in His timing.

This is the threefold vision that enables a cherished woman to fight for purity. First, she understands the heart of obedience. Second, she knows God's design for sex within marriage is for her good. And finally, she refuses to bow down to the gods of this world so that she can stand up for God's glory.

> Beloved, I urge you as aliens and strangers to abstain from fleshly lusts which wage war against the soul. Keep your behavior excellent among the Gentiles, so that in the thing in which they slander you as evildoers, they may because of your good deeds, as they observe them, glorify God in the day of visitation.
>
> 1 Peter 2:11–12 NASB

Don't you know that when you sleep with someone, your body makes a promise whether you do or not.

~ Julie Gianni (Cameron Diaz)
in *Vanilla Sky*

6

Detours

> Enter through the narrow gate. For wide is the gate and broad is the road that leads to destruction, and many enter through it. But small is the gate and narrow the road that leads to life, and only a few find it. ·
>
> —Jesus, Matthew 7:13–14

Pesky Little Orange Cones

Normally, I'm a pretty punctual person. But I'll admit, there are those times when I find myself racing through the house, grabbing my purse and sundry other random paraphernalia that I seem, for some odd reason, compelled to schlep to all my outings. When I'm finally loaded down like a bag lady, I jump into the car and play this little game I like to call Beat the Clock. Ah, who am I kidding? This scene describes how I roll most days.

I was running a tad bit late for a bridal shower, which I was über excited to attend since I was still reeling from a heart-wrenching breakup. Nothing says "happy bridesmaid" like swollen eyes with mascara running down your cheeks. But I digress . . . back to the shower. Ironically, it was showering—sheets of rain, to be precise. Houston was in the midst of a tropical storm, which had the city in gridlock. Pulling onto the freeway, I thought to myself, *Perrrrfectt! Not only am I running late, but apparently the whole city is, too!*

As I watched the minutes tick by on my dashboard, I felt hot anger stirring inside me. You know that feeling when your tummy begins to boil? Sensing my agitation, I thought, *What's the deal? Why am I getting frustrated?* Honestly, I'm not a woman prone to road rage. This was bigger than traffic. Something else was going on inside of me.

As I sat there for what seemed like an eternity, the source of my frustration dawned on me. My patience for waiting had reached its limit. The freeway gridlock felt all too similar to the gridlock happening in my personal life. Honestly, I was tired of waiting. It seemed that God had faithfully remembered all of my girlfriends and provided their "happily ever after," but somehow, mine was missing in action. Couple my impatience with the pain of a recent breakup, and I was one fed-up woman. *Waiting* was not a happy word for me.

As my frustration neared the boiling point, I looked to my right and noticed a small gap in the line of cars that revealed a construction zone that lay between the congested freeway and a wide-open, non-congested feeder road. A detour! How perfectly brilliant! All I needed to do was hop over one lane, cross the small construction zone, and free-sail my happy self all the way to the bridal shower.

A few friendly waves to the trucker in the lane beside me and I successfully scooted my SUV over the one lane and made a beeline through those pesky little orange cones blocking my way, then headed straight toward the construction zone. *Whew, I made it!*

No time for rejoicing. Only two seconds into my brilliant detour, I felt my car sink deep into mud. My "brilliant" detour proved not so smart. Due to the tropical storm, the construction zone was like quicksand, and I its first victim. What a total mess! Stuck in mud. And I thought I was late before . . .

This is a perfect example of how the Enemy tempts Christian women to forsake waiting for God's best. Most young women who know and love Jesus, if asked, would freely agree that sex outside of marriage is sin. Yet in the countless numbers I've surveyed, each woman can pinpoint a moment when she was tempted to detour from the path of obedience. A shortcut emerged, one they believed would enable them to attain the desire of their hearts faster than staying on God's path. Sure, they knew God had placed "orange cones" around sex, but those were ignored and they, too, raced past His protective warnings.

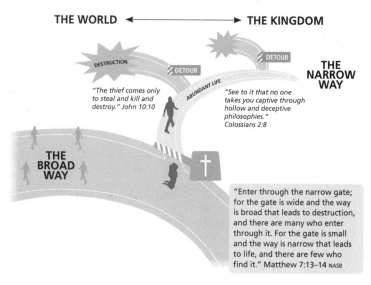

Let's back up for a minute and clarify an important truth. At some point in every Christian's life, he or she has made a choice to turn away from the world (depicted in the diagram above as the broad way) and trust Jesus as Savior. This is the salvation experience. Jesus described this moment as entering "through the narrow gate" (Matthew 7:13). This gate is described as "narrow" because there is only one way of salvation: faith in Jesus. As we enter into a relationship with God through Christ, we begin to follow Him in obedience along the narrow way, leading to abundant life. This is the walk of faith. The period between our salvation and when we see Jesus face-to-face is known as sanctification. To *sanctify* means to "make holy." Therefore, sanctification is the process whereby a Christian becomes more and more like Jesus in his or her affections, attitudes, and actions.

As we walk this narrow way, we will face temptations or tempting detours that seem like quick and easy shortcuts to our hearts' desire. These detours are Satan's schemes to turn us away from the abundant life. To clarify, while the Enemy knows we can never lose our salvation or our standing as children of God, he does have a clear agenda. Jesus spelled it out plainly for us in John 10:10: "The thief comes only to steal and kill and destroy."

How does he tempt us to turn away from the abundant life in Christ? Detours begin with the temptation to meet a legitimate need in an illegitimate way. Temptation whispers, "See this shortcut? If you turn here, you will reach the desire of your heart so much faster than taking that narrow road." Many travel the narrow road unaware of the deceptive detours along the path, only to realize they've been deceived after careening off the cliff.

Detoured

Recently, I taught a Bible study series on sexual purity for single Christian women. My goal in this teaching series was to equip women with a vision for sexual purity and to open their eyes to see the spiritual battle that rages all around them. A few days after the podcasts posted, our office began receiving emails. Testimony after testimony came in from women across the nation who confessed, "The mess I made of my life finally makes sense." They were able to see *how* and *why* they detoured from following Jesus and how the Enemy placed specific temptations along the way to satisfy their hearts' longing for love, security, or intimacy through sex.

One particular testimony caused me to wonder at how crafty our Enemy is in his schemes. I share her story as a prime example of how believing Satan's lies can lead to destruction.

I am one of those girls who believed Satan's lies and detoured from following Jesus toward an empty life filled with regret. This is my detour.

I was raised in a Christian home. As a little girl, I had faith in Jesus and believed the Gospel for salvation. My parents taught me that sex outside of marriage was morally wrong, and I knew this to be true. I wanted to be cherished. I wanted to be pure. But more than anything, I wanted to be loved.

Like many girls my age, I found my identity in guys' attention. My love bucket was temporarily filled up if a guy told me I was pretty. Sure, my parents set good boundaries for me; I wasn't allowed to date until I was sixteen, but I secretly started dating at age thirteen. By the time I was sixteen, I began a relationship that lasted until my senior year of college. I was head over heels.

About two months into our relationship, we started fooling around and going a little too far. I had my standards, but each time we were together, the lines were pushed. I was torn. On one hand, I knew sex outside of marriage was wrong, but on the other hand, I loved my boyfriend and was anxious that I would lose him. (By the way, I guess I should confess that my boyfriend was not a Christian.) I convinced myself it was okay to date him, and I even lied to my parents about his faith to get their approval. This was the first lie that Satan used to detour me. I was convinced I could lead my boyfriend to Jesus.

The longer we dated, the more he pressured me to have sex. I felt stupid for my faith, and he compared me to all the other girls in high school who were sleeping with their boyfriends. The Enemy whispered, "You are silly for holding on to your values." I felt dumb and old-fashioned. Since I didn't hold a vision for purity beyond just a "rule," I didn't really possess a solid reason to wait. Not only did I lack vision, but I also didn't know my identity in Christ—I was continually looking for guy attention to define my worth.

My defenses against the temptations were crumbling. My fear of not being loved grew stronger than my faith. At the time I couldn't see that his pressure was the exact opposite of love. Eventually, my fear of losing my boyfriend was so great that I gave in. I convinced myself that he loved me and we would get married one day, so sexual intimacy was "okay."

This is when the war against my soul began. The only way I can explain it is that by taking the detour, I found myself on a path far from God, and open to more and more of Satan's lies. First, I stopped going to church. The guilt and shame were too much. I was convinced I had to keep my sin in the dark or I would be rejected.

For example, in my freshman year of college I started visiting a campus ministry, but I felt like such a hypocrite that I stopped going altogether. The voice in my head said, "God will never forgive you. God will never love you." I did not feel worthy enough to even pray to God. My heart was so confused.

I missed my relationship with Jesus, but I couldn't break free from my boyfriend. I had heard that sex "superglues" you to the other person, and now I knew that to be true. I tried to convince myself that it was okay because we would get married after college. I had no idea how big of a lie that was until years later.

Even though I wasn't walking with the Lord, I still wanted my boyfriend to accept Christ. Sadly, the old cliché is true: My boyfriend pulled me down instead of me lifting him up. I didn't lead him to Jesus. Instead, he led me away from God. After a few years of my prodding him to go to church, he told me he didn't believe in Jesus. I knew then that I shouldn't be with him, but I didn't have the strength to break up with him. My soul was bonded to him.

During our senior year of college, he broke up with me. He said our lives were heading in different directions and that we possibly could get back together at some point "if our plans matched up." What in the world does that mean?

To say I was heartbroken is an understatement. I was completely devastated. I gave everything to him. My soul was one with him. I wrapped my identity up in him for so long that I didn't know who I was without him. It was at that point I realized the lie I had believed—"we are getting married . . . someday"—was a crock.

He didn't cherish me—not when we were sixteen or when we were twenty-two.

Looking back, I now see why God designed sex for the covenant of marriage. God wants us to feel secure and to not worry if the one we are giving ourselves to will be around in a couple of years. But back then I didn't understand the power of a covenant or how entrenched those lies were in my heart.

After we broke up, I changed my relationship status on Facebook to single, and guys started pursuing me. I loved it. The rush from the attention was amazing. My core heart issue was still the problem—I was looking for acceptance in guys' attention. But one thing was different. When I was sixteen, I wanted to remain pure for God and for my future husband. Now I didn't care. I thought it was too late. I didn't feel pure, so I didn't act it. Sex was always a part of these relationships because I believed yet another lie: "You're not a virgin anymore, so it doesn't matter." My sense of identity and worth was so jacked up. I had detoured so far from the truth that I was just lost—fumbling from one guy to the next.

By this point, I was in my senior year of college. I was a fraternity sweetheart, and the attention was like a drug. This only made my problem worse. My heart craved it, so I would do things with guys to hear them tell me things like, "You're so hot, smart, beautiful," "You're the perfect girl," etc. But after each hookup I was let down, feeling more shame and emptiness.

Addicted to male attention, I found myself constantly waiting for a text message from a guy to hang out. Honestly, I felt so disgusting. I realized that every time I went home with a guy, the only thing I wanted was affection, but I always ended up sleeping with him because I wanted to keep him around. My heart truly wanted to be cherished, yet I had believed so many lies that led me to just the opposite outcome.

One night my senior year of college, I hit rock bottom. I felt like trash. None of these guys treated me like a treasure, and with that realization, I began to sob. I faced my brokenness and took a hard look at the choices I was making. How did I detour so far from God's plan for my life?

For the first time in years, I opened my Bible. I felt led to Romans 5:8, which says, "God demonstrates his own love for us in this: While we were still sinners, Christ died for us."

Hot tears fell onto the pages of my Bible as the words "while we were still sinners" pierced my heart.

In my mess.

In my detour.

God still loved me.

God's truth was beginning to set me free.

I realized that I felt so unworthy to follow Jesus because of my sexual sin. Satan convinced me that God wouldn't take me back. But after reading that verse, I began to understand that God's grace really is amazing. I realized Jesus saw *all* of my sin when He went to the cross. Not just the sin from before my salvation, but also the sin I committed as a Christian. He knew I was going to stumble and fall, and He still died for me. He knew I would believe the lies, but He still paid the price to set me free from them. God's love began to break down my walls of shame. The cross was enough.

Even though I had chosen to turn away from Him, He never turned away from me. I continued to cry, but now my tears were those of regret: regret that I didn't believe God's truth sooner, regret that I didn't believe I was a treasure to be cherished, regret that I believed all those lies about sex.

But I get it now.

I know sexual sin is not God's best for me. If a man cherishes me, he will honor my purity. I know sex doesn't bring a girl the love, the security, and the acceptance she craves. That's just a big fat lie of the evil one.

Oh, and one more thing, I know who I am in Christ.

Redeemed.

Forgiven.

Cherished!

Choose Life

Detours can happen to any of us at any time. The temptation to barrel past the orange cones of life will entice all of us from time to time. But we must remember there is a payoff to following Christ. The Bible tells us repeatedly that God desires to bless us. Jeremiah 29:11 says, "For I know the plans I have for you . . . plans to prosper you and not to harm you, plans to give you hope and a future."

God does have a good plan and blessings for us, but we do face choices—temptations to detour—along the way. Jesus warned us about those detours when He said, "The thief comes only to steal and kill and destroy; I have come that they may have life, and have it to the full" (John 10:10).

The choice between two paths is a consistent theme throughout Scripture: the way of life via trusting and following God, or the way of destruction via believing Satan's deceptions. In the Bible, these two divergent paths are depicted through nature, real-life testimonies, and prophetic warnings.

For example, Psalm 1 contrasts these two paths by the type of life they produce.

Blessed is the one who does not walk in step with the wicked or stand in the way that sinners take or sit in the company of mockers, but whose delight is in the law of the LORD, and who meditates on his law day and night. That person is like a tree planted by

streams of water, which yields its fruit in season and whose leaf
does not wither—whatever they do prospers.

Psalm 1:1–3

Such vivid words to depict the contrast between these two paths!
One path is fruitful and prosperous, and the other path, well . . .

Not so the wicked! They are like chaff that the wind blows away.
Therefore the wicked will not stand in the judgment, nor sinners in
the assembly of the righteous. For the Lord watches over the way
of the righteous, but the way of the wicked leads to destruction.

Psalm 1:4–6

The life of the one who trusts God is fruitful and blessed. But the
one who walks away from God is described as "chaff." This word
is not common in our culture; it is an agriculture term describing
the part of a crop that is useless and is blown away by the wind.

The two paths are also illustrated in Scripture through real-life
testimonies of people who detoured. David detoured. Samson
detoured. Solomon detoured. The list goes on and on. And each
detour means the loss of what might have been—blessings, favor,
abundance. God's Word is given to us as a guide—to warn, to
equip, to instruct, and to encourage us as we grow in our relationship with Him. We study these biblical characters to see and
learn from their experiences how temptation lured each of them
down a path of destruction.

One such example is the nation of Israel. God rescued His
people out of slavery in Egypt through a series of miracles. Their
story beautifully parallels our redemption in Christ. Not only did
God rescue them from slavery, but His ultimate plan was to lead
them to the Promised Land—given this name because the Lord
promised it to their forefather, Abraham, generations before.

God has the same plan for you and me. He didn't simply rescue
us from sin. He intends to lead us into a land where we rest in His

promises and enjoy His blessings. As in Psalm 1, this land is depicted as a place of rich and bountiful blessing. For believers today, entering our "promised land" means experiencing the abundant life promised us in Christ and inheriting all the spiritual bounty we have as God's children. Israel's deliverance experience out of slavery and entrance into the Promised Land is a vivid example of our journey in trusting and following God.

In Deuteronomy 30, Israel stands on the precipice of entering their Promised Land. Prior to entering the land, God instructed Moses to divide the people into two groups. Half of the people recited the blessings that those who trust and follow God would receive, and the other half pronounced the curses that would befall those who turned away from God. Then Moses exhorted the people with these words:

> Look at what I've done for you today: I've placed in front of you Life and Good; Death and Evil. And I command you today: Love God, your God. Walk in his ways. Keep his commandments, regulations, and rules so that you will live, really live, live exuberantly, blessed by God, your God, in the land you are about to enter and possess. But I warn you: If you have a change of heart, refuse to listen obediently, and willfully go off to serve and worship other gods, you will most certainly die. You won't last long in the land that you are crossing the Jordan to enter and possess. I call Heaven and Earth to witness against you today: I place before you Life and Death, Blessing and Curse. Choose life so that you and your children will live. And love God, your God, listening obediently to him, firmly embracing him. Oh yes, he is life itself, a long life settled on the soil that God, your God, promised to give your ancestors, Abraham, Isaac, and Jacob.
>
> Deuteronomy 30:15–20 THE MESSAGE

Blessings or curses? Two paths lay before God's people. One way led to life and the other to death. God calls His people to "choose life"! The question before them as they stood on those mountains thousands of years ago and before us today is this: *Which way will we choose?*

When I imagine this scene, I think God is pleading with us, "I want to bless you and bring good things into your life. When you make the choice to believe me and to obey me—even when it's tough and even when you don't understand—you are choosing life itself."

The vision I hope to impart to you about sexual purity through this book is that when you choose to say no to temptation today, you are actually saying yes to God's very best in your future. Obedience always brings blessings. A yes to God's will is a yes to God's best.

Proverbs 14:12 says, "There is a way that appears to be right, but in the end it leads to death." As Christ-followers, we know our salvation is secure in Him. But we do make choices. Some reading this book have already tasted of the destruction that comes from living outside of God's will in the realm of sexual sin. You know you need to turn back. Others of you are facing temptation to turn away and walk in sexual sin. Some of you are choosing to walk in purity. Whatever our past, all of us will come to moments of temptation—we will face the option to detour. When you do stand at that crossroads, I pray you will hear the still, small voice of your loving heavenly Father say, "My cherished one, choose life!"

I'm just a girl, standing in front of a boy, asking him to love her.

~ Anna Scott (Julia Roberts)
in *Notting Hill*

7

Know Thy Enemy

> Satan gives Adam an apple, and takes away Paradise. Therefore in all temptations let us consider not what he offers, but what we shall lose.
>
> —Richard Sibbes, *A Puritan Golden Treasury*

Perhaps you are reading this book and are right now feeling defeated in the realm of sexual purity. Or maybe you're thinking you'll never meet a guy who will cherish you. Perhaps you are new to the Christian life and just plain scared to death of falling for the Enemy's schemes. Or maybe you've followed Jesus for years and fear a detour lies ahead. Trust me, I get it. I've been there. But I've also learned, as a former victim of Satan's deceptive schemes, how to fight and win.

Friends, in the Bible we learn about the spiritual warfare that rages over our God-given destinies. Sure, we discover that we do have an Enemy. But we can learn his mode of operation and grow in wisdom concerning his tactics and schemes. God, who is victorious, has equipped us with His Word so that we can be prepared for battle and stand in the victory that He already won for us. The first key to victory is to "know thy Enemy."

> No military commander could expect to be victorious in battle unless he understood his enemy. Should he prepare for an attack by land and ignore the possibility that the enemy might approach by air or by sea, he would open the way to defeat. Or should he prepare for a land and sea attack and ignore the possibility of an attack through the air, he would certainly jeopardize the campaign. No individual can be victorious against the adversary of our souls unless he understands that adversary; unless he understands his philosophy, his methods of operation, his methods of temptation.[1]
>
> —J. Dwight Pentecost, *Your Adversary, the Devil*

Game Film

I love Jesus. He is my Redeemer, my Healer, my Hope, and my Victory. The chief desire of my heart is to glorify His name. For this reason, I loathe devoting any attention or time to discussing our Enemy. But after hearing countless stories of crushed hearts and crushed lives, I know I must speak up and equip a generation that longs to be cherished. The only reason I write these words is to expose Satan's tactics so that you can stand firm when facing his deceptive schemes.

In Texas, where I grew up, football is a pretty big deal. Whether it's Friday night lights or college game day or cheering for the Dallas Cowboys, we love football. While I'm 100 percent Grade A girl, I do know a thing or two about the game. It's in the DNA. Here's a football fact: Whenever a team prepares to face an opponent, they watch game film of the opposing team. In order to win, they must study the offense, learn the defense, and understand the opponent's strategy. As women of God who long to be cherished, we must do the same.

My goal in this chapter is to equip you with "game film" of our Enemy in action. We will examine how he operated in the past so that we are trained for victory in the future. It doesn't matter if you've failed in the arena of sexual purity over and over again or if you're a girl who has never faced a battle, you can begin today to stand . . . to fight . . . to resist . . . and to walk in victory. Your destiny is not determined by your past; your destiny is determined by your God.

The Bible gives our Enemy many names: the devil, Satan, Lucifer. He is also known by his deeds: thief, deceiver, liar, accuser, destroyer, and tempter—just to name a few. I suppose the big question is *Why?* Why does Satan seek to deceive and destroy us? For that answer, we must go back to the beginning, back to his origin, to understand our Enemy's true motive.

Before Time Began

Before time began, God existed: uncreated, unformed, unblemished, undivided. *One in Essence yet three in Person.* Christians across the globe call this divine mystery the Trinity. We believe in one God: Father, Son, and Holy Spirit—three in One—united in perfect harmony and holiness.

The Bible reveals to us that God is Self-Existent—without need of anyone or anything. Yet bursting forth from the divine perfection, God created all things. Why? Theologians debate the ultimate *why*, but the Bible reveals over and over again, God's purpose in creating was to display His glorious splendor.

One of my all-time favorite Scripture passages testifies to this purpose:

> Christ is the visible image of the invisible God. He existed before anything was created and is supreme over all creation, for through him God created everything in the heavenly realms and on earth.

He made the things we can see and the things we can't see—such as thrones, kingdoms, rulers, and authorities in the unseen world. Everything was created through him and for him.

Colossians 1:15–16 NLT

Satan is a created being. But let me be crystal clear: He is not God, nor is he equal with God. Originally, he was an angel in heaven's court, one of the most beautiful creations. His purpose was to praise and point to the beauty and glory of God Most High. Instead, Satan's heart grew proud and he desired praise for himself.

Author Mary DeMuth, in her book *Beautiful Battle*, perfectly captures the moment that everything changed for and within Satan:

> Something shifted in a hiccup of a moment. A slight reorientation of the gaze from God's splendor to his own. Every day the amount of time spent gazing at God ebbed in light of Satan's newfound affection for himself, his beauty, his power. He may have reasoned, *Surely there is a place in this kingdom for more than one God.* He sowed discontent among other angelic servants, plotting to set up his own kingdom where the servants would follow him, revere him, extol his beauty.[2]

Full of his own pride, he desired worship for himself. He desired a kingdom where he would be worshiped and praised. The Bible records the extent of his evil ambition in Isaiah 14, where Satan boasts, "I will raise my throne above the Most High God." Satan waged a war in heaven and lost. As a result, he and the one-third of the angels who fought on his side were expelled. These fallen angels are now referred to in the Bible as demons, powers, authorities, or evil spirits. They are powerful, evil, angelic hosts that carry out Satan's schemes. Satan is thoroughly evil, despises God and all that is good, and is set on destroying all that God has made.[3]

The War Against the Image Bearers

This is Satan's history, but to understand the nature of the spiritual war around us and how to stand against our Enemy, we must first delve back into our own origin. For in our history we discover why this Enemy seeks to destroy us.

> Then God said, "Let the earth produce every sort of animal, each producing offspring of the same kind—livestock, small animals that scurry along the ground, and wild animals." And that is what happened. God made all sorts of wild animals, livestock, and small animals, each able to produce offspring of the same kind. And God saw that it was good.
>
> Then God said, "Let us make human beings in our image, to be like us. They will reign over the fish in the sea, the birds in the sky, the livestock, all the wild animals on the earth, and the small animals that scurry along the ground."
>
> So God created human beings in his own image.
>
> In the image of God he created them; male and female he created them.
>
> Then God blessed them and said, "Be fruitful and multiply. Fill the earth and govern it. Reign over the fish in the sea, the birds in the sky, and all the animals that scurry along the ground."
>
> Then God said, "Look! I have given you every seed-bearing plant throughout the earth and all the fruit trees for your food. And I have given every green plant as food for all the wild animals, the birds in the sky, and the small animals that scurry along the ground—everything that has life." And that is what happened.
>
> Then God looked over all he had made, and he saw that it was very good!
>
> And evening passed and morning came, marking the sixth day.
>
> Genesis 1:24–31 NLT

The opening lines of Scripture record the creation of the world. After speaking forth solar systems and oceans, butterflies and beaches, God turns His attention to the pinnacle of His creation—humankind. This time, God's handiwork is not just "good," but "very good." We also see that when God fashioned humanity, He made us in His image (Genesis 1:26).

We are image bearers, created to reflect the glory of our Creator. Just as the moon reflects the light of the sun, so we, too, were designed to reflect the glory of God. Originally, God placed the human race in a beautiful garden—Eden—which He filled with everything they needed for a life of joy, peace, and purpose. Unparalleled beauty. Ultimate bliss. Everything in Eden was good for Adam, except for one thing: The Tree of Knowledge of Good and Evil. This particular tree was off-limits. God told Adam not to eat of it, for if he did, he would die (Genesis 2:16–17).

After forming Adam from the dust of the ground and breathing His very breath of life into him, the Lord said, "It is not good for the man to be alone." God then fashioned the woman and presented her to Adam (Genesis 2:18–22).

Cue Eve.

Adam's response is one of explosive joy.

> "At last!" the man exclaimed. "This one is bone from my bone, and flesh from my flesh! She will be called 'woman,' because she was taken from 'man.'"
>
> Genesis 2:23 NLT

Ladies, grab a tissue. It's time for the very first wedding.

A simple garden ceremony.

One man.

One woman.

One Witness.

A sacred covenant sealed with two bodies, naked and not ashamed.

God's Word comments on this holy moment, "For this reason a man shall leave his father and his mother, and be joined to his wife; and they shall become one flesh" (Genesis 2:24 NASB). *One flesh.* Two souls, under His approving gaze, became one. *This is marriage.* This is God's beautiful design. This is a divine mystery. As Neil T. Anderson rightly points out, "Here we see that God's ideal plan for marriage was outlined in the garden before sin entered the world: one man and one woman forming an inseparable union and living in dependence on God."[4]

Adam and Eve couldn't comprehend depression, disease, destruction, divorce, or death. Connected to their Life-Source, they were whole and complete. Yet this idyllic bliss was shattered when Satan entered the scene.

Let's recap. Whose image does Satan hate the most? That's right, the Lord God Almighty. Therefore, he unleashes on God's image bearers—the human race—the full brunt of his jealous fury. Yet notice how our Enemy operates. (Cherished ones, pay close attention to this game film.) Satan doesn't run in with guns blazing, screaming loud threats at the two image bearers. No, he is subtle. Cunning. Sly. Satan slithers up to Eve in the form of a serpent.

He uses words . . .

He uses suggestion . . .

He uses lies . . .

And when those lies were believed . . . the ultimate detour occurred.

Satan's M.O.

The best way for us to study game film of our Enemy is to return to the scene of the original detour—Satan's temptation of Eve in Genesis 3:1–6. Here we see that his attack reveals careful craftiness and cunning. We glean from this interaction how he operates in doubt, denial, and deception, which result ultimately in destruction.

The serpent was clever, more clever than any wild animal God had made. He spoke to the Woman: "Do I understand that God told you not to eat from any tree in the garden?" The Woman said to the serpent, "Not at all. We can eat from the trees in the garden. It's only about the tree in the middle of the garden that God said, 'Don't eat from it; don't even touch it or you'll die.'" The serpent told the Woman, "You won't die. God knows that the moment you eat from that tree, you'll see what's really going on. You'll be just like God, knowing everything, ranging all the way from good to evil." When the Woman saw that the tree looked like good eating and realized what she would get out of it—she'd know everything!—she took and ate the fruit and then gave some to her husband, and he ate.

Genesis 3:1–6 The Message

Phase 1: Doubt

Satan began his temptation of Eve with what appeared to be a simple question. Yet hidden within this question was a poisonous pill called doubt. He approached Eve in a friendly manner and sought to draw her into a dialogue: "Has God indeed said, 'You shall not eat of every tree of the garden'?"

By phrasing the question in this manner, Satan does two things. First, he implies he is concerned about her welfare. Second, by zeroing in on the commandment, he shifts the focus away from God's gracious *provision* (the abundant and rich bounty of the garden) to get Eve to focus on God's one *prohibition* (i.e., the forbidden fruit). Satan plants a seed of doubt in Eve's heart against God's Word. His objective was to get Eve to think that God's command was unreasonable and unfair.[5]

This reveals how Satan works to tempt us into sexual sin—or any sin for that matter. Satan begins by planting seeds of doubt. Typically, a Christian woman knows God's design for sex is marriage, but doubts begin to creep into her mind. These thoughts are primarily targeted at God's character. If Satan can convince us that God isn't good, then he can easily lead us to forsake God's commands.

Oftentimes, when a woman is dealing with a hurt or disappointment, Satan whispers, "If God loved you, He wouldn't allow this to happen." When the doubts about God's goodness take root, our hearts are open to entertain Satan's other lies and suggestions. This is why we are told in Scripture to "take captive every thought" (2 Corinthians 10:5). For it is through the gateway of our minds that the Enemy enters to wage war against our souls.

Phase 2: Denial

He's a crafty little devil. In phase one, Satan pretended to be compassionate toward Eve and concerned for her welfare as a ruse to gain her trust so he could engage her in dialogue. Once his goal was accomplished, he planted the seed of doubt. In phase two, he is not so subtle. Now he directly denies the truthfulness of God's Word. "The serpent said to the woman, 'You surely will not die'" (Genesis 3:4 NASB). Don't miss this: Satan just called God a liar. He downplays the consequence of disobedience and thereby calls into question God's truthfulness. By telling Eve that she would not die, he essentially said she shouldn't believe God.

I recall when dating my husband that for a few weeks, a certain thought would flutter through my mind. The thought was, *Does the Bible actually say that sex before marriage is a sin?* Normally, I'd laugh to myself and say, *Yes, of course,* and move on about my day. What I noticed is that, over a few weeks, this question fluttered through in various forms.

Then one night when Justin leaned over to kiss me goodnight, those thoughts rushed at me, demanding, *Did God really say . . . ?*

The power of the doubt was shocking.

I knew better.

But I had a firsthand look at just how powerfully Satan's seed of doubt could grow into weeds of disobedience.

Realizing I was in a moment of weakness, I quickly said goodnight and ran to my car. Girls, the Bible says to "flee temptation," and that's exactly what I did. I ran! I didn't trust myself and knew I was in a battle.

Once at my house, I thought back over the moments and weeks leading up to that night. How little by little my reliance on God's Word was being undermined. How the questions popped up, out of nowhere, suggesting that perhaps, just perhaps, God didn't really *say* sex before marriage was sin. These thoughts seemed so innocent that I just ignored them, but looking back now, I see them for what they were—Satan's usual tricks.

The primary issue in phase two is authority. *Authority* is defined as "power to influence or command thought, opinion, or behavior."[6] I'll be the first to admit, *authority* is not a fun word. It reeks of rules and not-so-fun images of discipline. But I'd like to lay aside those images for a moment and evaluate the importance of authority in our lives.

As human beings, we have a choice of authority. We can either submit our lives to God and His word as the defining truth, or we can rely on ourselves and our "feelings" as our guide. The first way is the way of life; the second is the way of destruction.

Our culture promotes the authority of self and feelings as supreme. The mantra "follow your heart" is the warm and fuzzy notion depicted in romantic comedies that says our hearts will lead us in the right direction. I don't want to offend anyone with this next statement, but honestly, that thinking is straight from the pit of hell. Our feelings are fickle. Our emotions cannot be trusted as a reliable guide.

One of the very first verses I memorized as a new Christian taught me this truth:

> Trust in the Lord with all your heart and lean not on your own understanding; in all your ways submit to him, and he will make your paths straight.
>
> Proverbs 3:5–6

This verse speaks of authority. As God's children, we are called to trust Him and rely on His Word as our guide. This verse explicitly warns us not to "lean on [our] own understanding." Imagine someone with a broken leg leaning on a crutch. This image helps us understand what this proverb is calling us to do. To *lean* means to rely, to put your weight upon, or to rest.[7] When we "lean on our own understanding," we are relying on what we feel or think to determine our decisions. Scripture warns us that when faced with choices or decisions, how we "feel" is not always the best indicator of what we should "do."

Thankfully, God did not leave us here to figure out things on our own. In His great love for us, He gave us His Word, the Bible, as our authority and our guide. Psalm 119:105 says, "Your word is a lamp for my feet, a light on my path." What does this have to do with the battle over sexual purity? Think back to how Satan detoured Eve. First, he caused her to doubt God's goodness, and then he questioned the authority of God's command by asking, "Did God really say . . . ?" In this challenge, he sought to undermine what the Lord had spoken.

This undermining of God's authority is precisely what Satan does with us today. Our Enemy doesn't want us to trust and rely on God's Word, but rather, he wants us to trust our feelings and rely on ourselves. When we think thoughts like *Is sex outside of marriage really sin?* we are questioning the authority of God's Word to lead and guide us.

John MacArthur writes, "Every temptation, directly or indirectly, is the temptation to doubt and distrust God."[8] For a Christian woman living in a romantic-comedy world where decisions are based on the idiom "If it feels good, do it," we must willingly submit ourselves to what God has spoken as the determiner of right and wrong. Therefore, when faced with temptation, we can resist the Enemy with the truth of God's Word.

Phase 3: Deception

I personally think this final phase is his specialty. After planting his seeds of doubt and denying the authority of God's Word, Satan now begins to distort truth in order to deceive Eve into disobedience. After telling Eve that God is a liar, and that sin will not result in death, Satan next explains *why* God has lied. "For God knows that in the day you eat from it your eyes will be opened, and you will be like God, knowing good and evil" (Genesis 3:5 NASB). Satan essentially tells Eve that God lies to her because He does not want her to have all the wonderful blessings that come with eating the forbidden fruit. This statement is a direct attack on the character of God. His hatred and jealousy of the Lord is barely veiled as he attacks God's motive and insinuates that evil intentions lie behind God's prohibition of the fruit. He deceives Eve into thinking that God is selfish in His command and is ultimately not good, thereby undermining her trust, allegiance, and relationship.

The issue of trust is huge in our fight for sexual purity. Let's face it. If we don't trust God or believe that He is good, then why on earth would we ever want to honor Him with our bodies or wait for His best? Satan knows the power of striking when our defenses are down. For this reason, one of the most vulnerable times in our lives is when we are in pain. In our sadness, heartaches, and unmet desires, Satan slithers in with his deceptions.

I'm mentoring a young woman right now who loves God and wants to walk in purity. Her past is similar to my own, in that she was sexually active before trusting Christ. We talked yesterday, and I learned that she and her boyfriend recently broke up. Knowing her story and knowing her pain, but most of all knowing how our Enemy operates, I told her, "You need to be on your guard against temptation right now. Your heart is wounded, and Satan loves to deceive God's daughters in moments like these." She admitted that she was already feeling weak, and we prayed for her to stand firm in her faith . . . even through this heartbreak.

Let me pull the curtain back and reveal Satan's master plan. He wants to convince us that God isn't good and we shouldn't trust Him because it will leave us susceptible to temptation. In moments of unmet desire, heartbreak, or grief, Satan sends a poisonous arrow of doubt straight at your heart. This was his plan with Eve. He persuaded her to think God was "holding out on her" and that she would be better off not listening to Him.

The final step in this deception is to convince Eve of the reward she will receive in rebellion. "When you eat from it your eyes will be opened, and you will be like God, knowing good and evil" (Genesis 3:5). Satan proposed to Eve the same dark motive that led to his own fall: independence from God. His words suggested . . .

You don't need to rely on God.

You can have equality with God.

You can decide for yourself what is right and what is wrong.

Satan paraded the forbidden fruit before Eve as perfectly harmless, and he portrayed the Lord as selfish and mean for His prohibition. His mode of operation has not changed since the beginning. Satan loves to convince men and women that God is withholding pleasure from them and that the only route to happiness is to detour into sin. He entices us to crave things outside of God's stated provision and justifies the temptation by undermining our belief in God's character and His Word.

Sam Storms illustrates the three-step process of doubt, denial, and deception by personifying how sin whispers in our ears:

Sin comes to us, taps us on the shoulder or tugs at our shirttail and whispers in our ear: "You deserve better than what God has provided. He's holding out on you. You deserve to feel good about yourself. I'll affirm you in a way no one else can. Why live in misery any longer? Come to me. I'll give you a sense of power you've never known before. I'll expand your influence. I'll fill your heart with a sense of accomplishment. I'll nourish your soul. You've never had a physical rush like the one I've got in store for you. Obeying God is boring. It's a pain. He's always telling you to do stuff that's difficult and burdensome and inconvenient or ordering you to forsake the few things that really bring you happiness. Come on. You've only got one life. Obedience is ugly. My way is fun. My way feels good."[9]

I hope you noticed how the seductive voice causes doubt, denial, and deception. Understanding this gives us discernment into our own battles.

Now we have reviewed game film on our Enemy and are wise to how he operates. Next, we will investigate the specific lies Satan uses to seduce us into sexual sin and how we can wield the sword of the Spirit to defeat him.

We are all programmed to believe that if a guy acts like a total jerk that means he likes you.

~ Gigi Phillips (Ginnifer Goodwin)
in *He's Just Not That Into You*

8

The Battleground

Satan's primary strategy for controlling your life is by infiltrating your mind.

—Robert Jeffress, *The Divine Defense*

When I say I can't begin to count the number of weddings I have been in, I am not exaggerating. I've worn my share of taffeta. I've danced to Beyonce's "Single Ladies" while some overzealous groomsman ushered (or rather, pushed) me to the dance floor for my all-time favorite event (insert eye roll)—the humiliating bouquet toss. I've now worn every color in the rainbow as a bridesmaid and read most of Paul's epistles in my new preferred role, the "official" Scripture reader. Yet in all of my wedding memories, one moment will always stand out as the I-can't-believe-that-just-happened-to-me moment of all.

A good friend decided to have her wedding in beautiful Cabo San Lucas, Mexico. Attending this one was a no-brainer. Seriously, three days of sun and sand was not a big sacrifice for me.

So I boarded the plane for Cabo with my maid-of-honor checklist and a beach bag full of mindless reading. The wedding was breathtaking: white sand, crystal blue water, and the absolutely stunning bride standing before her groom at sunset. Yet all of these images were trumped by a single unscripted one.

So there I stood, poised next to the bride, holding my bouquet at my belly button, my feet aching in my three-inch heels, as the tide rolled in just steps away from us. Taking in the seriousness of the covenant ceremony, I listened intently as the pastor spoke about our awesome God, who is Creator of all things . . . oceans, stars, animals, the birds of the air, and of course, marriage.

I kid you not, at the precise moment the pastor said, "The birds of the air," a huge sea gull, as if hearing his cue, decided to be a tad bit dramatic and interrupted the ceremony by swooping down and perching himself right on my perfectly coifed updo.

I so wish this were fiction. Alas, it is not. For some reason, Mr. Angry Bird picked *me* out of everyone to sink his talons into. I can only assume he confused the mounds of bobby pins and hairspray for a suitable nest. I'm pretty sure the most memorable part of the wedding for all in attendance is me wildly flapping my arms and dancing around in order to shoo the bird off my head.

By now, you might be scratching your own head, trying to make a connection between an unfortunate encounter with a bird and the battle we face over sexual purity. I divulge this very embarrassing tale because this experience perfectly illustrates the nature of temptation. As Martin Luther said, "You can't prevent a bird from flying over your head, but you can keep it from building a nest in your hair."

Luther's point is this: Everyone is tempted to sin. Temptation itself is not sin, but acting upon it is. The fact that you picked up this book or downloaded it to your e-reader clues me in: You are probably already well aware that Christians are not immune to the lure of sexual sin. The nature of our battle lies in our struggle to resist the Enemy's detours and walk the narrow way that leads to abundant life.

Just think about it. I did nothing to cause or invite that sea gull to come after me during the wedding. But I did have a choice. It was up to me whether Mr. Angry Bird would build a nest in my updo. As Christians, we have a choice whether to yield to the temptations we face.

Temptation

We begin by answering the all-important question, *What is temptation?* Pastor John MacArthur said, "Every temptation, directly or indirectly, is the temptation to doubt and distrust God."[1] As we learned in the previous chapter, this has always been Satan's mode of operation. When he tempted Eve in the garden with the forbidden fruit, his lie was about God's character, insinuating that God was holding out on her. He tempts us in the same way with the deceitful thought or an idea that says, "God cannot be trusted."

In many ways, sex outside of marriage is presented as a tasty "forbidden fruit," and God is depicted as the cruel withholder of our pleasure. Satan taunts, "Obedience to God's command keeps you from the desires of your heart. True happiness can be found in this detour."

While researching for this book, I interviewed Christian women of all ages concerning their battle for sexual purity. As I read their confessions, I discovered seven common lies used to detour women into sexual sin. These temptations take the form of justifications—patterns of thinking that wear down resistance and entice us to take a shortcut to meet our longings and desires. These are so common that when I meet someone who is struggling with sexual sin, I can easily trace her defeat back to one of these lies.

I write these to expose how our Enemy operates so that you can recognize them when you hear them and learn to resist.

In the previous chapter, we learned that Jesus described Satan as the Father of Lies. Knowing this to be true, we have insight into how he operates and how we can stand against his schemes. In *Renovation of the Heart*, Dallas Willard writes:

> Ideas and images are, accordingly, the primary focus of Satan's efforts to defeat God's purposes with and for humankind. . . . When he undertook to draw Eve away from God, he did not hit her with a stick, but with an idea. It was the idea that God could not be trusted and that she must act on her own to secure her own well-being. This is the basic idea behind all temptation. God is presented as depriving us by his commands of what is good, so we think we must take matters into our own hands and act contrary to what he has said. . . . This image of God leads us to pushing him out of our thoughts . . . and putting ourselves on the throne of the universe.[2]

Reflecting on my own battle for sexual purity, I can clearly see which of Satan's lies crept in. At first I didn't shoo them away but allowed them to make a nest in my mind. After a few weeks, when the temptations grew stronger and stronger and resisting seemed futile, I knew I was in trouble.

Thankfully, while praying for strength to resist temptation, God spoke to my heart and reminded me of Proverbs 23:7, which says, "For as he thinks within himself, so he is" (NASB). This verse contains a powerful truth, which proves our first key to resisting temptation: We must think about *what we think about*. The Lord equipped me with a powerful tool for resisting detours: *recognize the lie!*

Remember my unpleasant detour into the mud? When waiting in traffic that day, I reasoned that I would arrive faster at my destination if I drove through a banned area. Ignoring the bright orange cones, I barreled past reason and wound up in a huge mess. Reflecting on my mishap, I realize that the highway department was only looking out for my best interest in placing those barriers on the freeway. They knew the construction zone was not fit for driving. Yet I chose to believe a lie—a lie that said, "Just ignore that cone. Nothing bad will happen if you take this shortcut. You're in a huge hurry, so it's okay."

The same is true with sexual sin. God clearly states in His Word that sex is designed for marriage. His "orange cones" tell us what is safe and good versus what is unsafe and destructive. Looking back, I now realize that I was falling for those same lies the Enemy uses to detour us all. I'm thankful the Lord spoke to me in the midst of this struggle and helped me to recognize that I was in danger. By allowing the thoughts to take root in my mind, my resolve was weakening. The Enemy was winning the battle for my mind. Thankfully, once I recognized his lies, I picked up my sword and began to fight.

The Lies We Believe

The film *Catch Me If You Can*, starring Leonardo DiCaprio, is the true story of Frank Abagnale, a young man who becomes one of the greatest con men of all time. Abagnale specialized in check fraud and successfully evaded the FBI and every other government agency for years as he deceived banks and officials across the globe.

Years and millions of dollars later, Abagnale was finally brought to justice. Ironically, he now works on the side of the law as a top consultant on preventing forgery and designing secure checking systems. He's the best. He can spot a fraud faster than anyone, since he spent years studying the real thing and knows firsthand how thieves think.

Just as Frank Abagnale is superb at spotting a fraud, we, too, must grow in our discernment and ability to detect the lies Satan uses to lead us into temptation. Recognizing the lies we believe is key to winning the battle for our minds and ultimately the war for sexual purity.

Lie #1: "But We Are in Love . . . So It's Okay"

I did everything with my high school boyfriend. Everything from my first kiss to losing my virginity. For the first two years of dating, I said that I didn't want to have sex until marriage, but I was so in love I thought it was okay, and I gave in after that.

—age 24

Even though I was a Christian, I began to rationalize and told myself that when I fell in love, sex would be okay. Two months after we began dating, he told me he loved me, and a month later I was sleeping with him.

—age 18

The Enemy has worked hard to convince the masses through television, movies, music, and other media that "love" is the new standard of sexual purity. Before you think I'm hyper-opposed to media, let me clarify: I'm not. Like any girl, I love a good sitcom, and I can get absolutely engrossed in a great movie, but I'm fully aware of the power of media to influence my thinking and thereby my choices. Therefore, I watch with discernment.

I recognize how impressionable our minds are by what we see and hear. Movies and sitcoms portray beautiful young couples falling into bed within minutes of falling "in love." As women, we aspire to the fairy tale, and the more these scenes are paraded before the theater of our minds, the more we normalize the behavior. Sadly, most of the time in these films, "love" proves a fickle emotion that changes on a whim. Love could be one wild night in Vegas or one romantic weekend at the beach. Marriage is not even on the radar. The more these images and plots fill our minds, the more we equate love and sex instead of sex and marriage.

Hands down, the number one lie women believe to justify sex outside of marriage is the excuse "But we are in love." Over time, the constant influence of culture wears down resistance, and women succumb to the lie that sex equals love. The truth is, in reality, sex often just equals lust.

Love seeks the best for the other person. Lust seeks what pleases self. A man who loves a woman will not use her to gratify his sexual desires apart from a covenant, and likewise, a woman who loves a man will not use her body to entice him into sin. Ladies, I must be very clear here: A man who truly loves you will wait. The opposite is also true: A selfish man will pressure you, and he certainly will not cherish you.

I can bring my own experience to testify on this one. As I think back to my life before Christ, to the men I was sexually involved with, not one of those guys truly loved me. Sure, they may have liked me or even desired me—but love, that is another story. Love seeks *the best* for the other person. In those "relationships," I ended up feeling more like a commodity to be used than a woman to be cherished. Compare that experience with my relationship with my husband. His love motivated him to restrain his own physical desires in order to honor me and to protect our future marriage. Sacrificial love is what Jesus modeled for us. Christ laid aside His own comfort and pleasure in order to love and cherish us.

This morning as Justin was walking out the door to go to work, I stopped him and asked, "What was your motivation in waiting until we were married for sex? Was it just obedience to God's command, or was there a different reason?" He paused, looked away to think about it, and then said, "Every guy wants to have sex, that's a given. But I wanted the best for me and for you. I knew sex outside of marriage would be temporarily satisfying, but it would be destructive to you, to me, and to our future marriage. Honestly, no one truly knows if they are with 'the one' until they are standing at that altar, in front of God, making a covenant. So whenever I was tempted, I focused on the future instead of the present. The long-term consequences outweighed the potential of momentary pleasure."

Cherished ones, that is the huge difference between lust and love. Lust demands immediate satisfaction. Lust screams "Right now!" On the other hand, true love waits, for it will forgo momentary pleasure to ensure a future blessing. A man who loves a woman will wait and honor her. Love is often used to justify sex before marriage, but ironically, what is revealed proves to be the opposite of love. If someone loves the other person, they will seek the best for that person.

Lie #2: "But We Are Getting Married . . . Someday"

While dating my husband, we set our boundaries early on and decided that kissing was our limit. But in the heat of the moment, when it was at the point that we could stick with our boundaries or push the line a little bit, one thing I would hear was, "This feels so good and I'm with someone I can see myself marrying, so it's okay." Really, my fleshly desire completely surpassed my desire for purity and righteousness.

—age 28

My relationship with my college boyfriend was a sexual one. Even though I was a Christian, we still slept together. I justified it by thinking we would get married after college. When we broke up my senior year, I was so overwhelmed with the pain of the breakup and the regret that I had been so naïve.

—age 25

Time after time, when I counsel Christian women who are struggling with sexual sin, one of the most common statements

I hear is this: "I justified sex because I thought we were getting married." Sadly, this one is believed by girls as young as middle school and by single women well past middle age. The majority of the time, women share their story with me, through tears, after the major breakup has transpired.

Satan is the great justifier. Trust me, I've heard all the lies. For the record, "getting married" and "being married" are not the same thing. A couple is married when they stand before God and commit their lives to one another. I can't explain it. Honestly, I don't know how it works, but I do know that something supernatural takes place in a covenant ceremony.

Sex outside of the marriage covenant between two unmarried people is called fornication. Yep, I just went old-school and pulled out the big F word. Seriously, though, the Bible is crystal clear. (See 1 Corinthians 6:18, Galatians 5:19–21, Hebrews 13:4, 1 Thessalonians 4:3–4, and Ephesians 5:3.) Fornication, defined as sexual intimacy with anyone other than your covenant spouse, is sin; not only is it breaking God's holy law, but it damages a person—body, mind, soul, and spirit. And God loves us too much to permit such destruction.

Not only does soul damage happen to the person engaging in sex before marriage, but seeds of destruction are sown in the relationship. In the moment, it may feel just fine—great, even. But just as a seed is planted in the ground and sprouts fruit months later, when sin is planted, it bears its own fruit in the future.

Donna Lee Schillinger, editor of *Purity's Big Payoff/Premarital Sex Is a Big Rip-off* writes,

> Sex outside of marriage is like a delicious meal fully enjoyed, despite the fact that it is swarming with salmonella microorganisms. Just as poisoned food can taste very good but will surely leave us in pain, abusing the gift of sex feels great while it's happening, but will make us regrettably ill later on, as the experience digests itself in our lives and souls.[3]

Food poisoning is an excellent illustration to explain how sexual sin can feel fine in the moment but have long-term consequences. A close friend of mine shared with me the heartache, mistrust, and pain that premarital sex has caused to her marriage. Not only did they as a couple have to deal with the other "lovers" still lingering in their marriage bed, but the sin from their dating relationship bore fruit many years into their married life. They faced years of counseling and stood at the pinnacle of divorce due to choices made in "the heat of the moment."

I've heard countless testimonies from women who did, in fact, marry men with whom they were sexually active prior to marriage. In moments of vulnerability they confess how the seeds of destruction bore bitter fruit years into the marriage . . . fruit of jealousy, insecurity, and shame. It is my heartfelt belief that God is good and He desires the absolute best for us. His commandments are to protect us. He wants our marriages free from these bitter fruits. When we choose to believe God and abstain from sex prior to marriage, then we are setting ourselves up for the best possible future.

Lie #3: "Sex Is Not That Big of a Deal"

I remember while kissing my boyfriend I would think "just go ahead and let him go further this time." The longer we made out and the more the temptation increased, the more I would think, "Is sex outside of marriage really a sin?" These doubts about God's Word would bombard me until my defenses were weak. The temptation seemed to be no big deal. I actually got to the point where I didn't feel guilty at all. Even though I was a Christian, I convinced myself that sex outside of marriage wasn't something I should even feel guilty about. Now I know how very wrong I was.

—age 22

I've encountered many reactions and responses to my sex talks. After hearing my testimony of life before Jesus, how sexual promiscuity was the detour that sent me down a path of destruction, some women are visibly angry. What elicits such anger? For one thing, our culture bristles at any mention of sexual standards, and these women feel that I have "no right to tell anyone what is right or wrong." While there are girls who are angry, others just laugh—at me and with each other, at what most perceive to be an archaic view of sexuality. They tell themselves they are "having fun" in the party scene and don't want to hear anything that would spoil their good time.

There are others in the room, though, who are listening. Leaning in, turning away from distractors, because they know. Their souls know that what I am saying is truth . . . and they are thirsting desperately for truth that will set them free.

There are many reactions and responses to a sex talk. I've seen the full gamut: anger, laughter, tears, apathy, and hope. At one point in every talk, every woman in the room is with me. It's the moment when I begin to describe God's glorious plan for sex: covenant, intimacy, oneness, bonding, mystery.

The women who were once angry are now listening. They've never heard this before. The laughter has ceased, the room grows quiet, still. With their defense mechanisms forsaken, their souls are laid bare, honest. They can't deny it; they do want God's best.

God's design is intriguing; more than that, it is enticing. Now they have vision. They want something better. Tired of settling, they know their souls are battered and bruised. They can't deny the truth anymore. . . . Sex *is* a really big deal.

Many have experienced the consequences of sex outside of marriage, and it doesn't take much talking to convince them of these, but most of the women had no idea there was an alternative. Most assumed that popular culture is right, sex is "no big deal." Satan's lies that downgrade sex are so rampant. At every turn we are inundated with messages that degrade sex from the sacred to the common. This lie rears its ugly head in times of temptation.

Satan is masterful at minimizing consequences. He paints scenarios that lead us to think obedience is unnecessary and that we won't experience any negative side effect if we detour. Think back to the game film we reviewed in the last chapter. This particular lie is a great example of Satan's M.O. He undermines our belief in God's Word in order to deceive us. Therefore, many women believe the lie that sex isn't a big deal. But studies from renowned psychologists and physicians reveal the truth: What we do with our bodies does affect our souls. While sex may not always affect a person physically with an STD or an unplanned pregnancy, it does affect a person emotionally and psychologically.

Dr. Miriam Grossman is a psychiatrist and author of the groundbreaking book *Unprotected*, which exposes the destructive consequences that sexual promiscuity causes to the emotional stability of women. The title of the book is very telling. While students are instructed to protect themselves with condoms to prevent disease, these do nothing to protect the heart. What she sees in her profession is the blatant truth that a condom cannot prevent the damage done to a woman's identity and esteem. She notes:

> In a study of 6,500 adolescents, sexually active teenage girls were more than three times more likely to be depressed, and nearly three times as likely to have had a suicide attempt, than girls who were not sexually active.[4]

As a psychiatrist on a university campus for many years, Grossman witnessed firsthand the depression, dependency, and disease that resulted from the widespread belief in society that sex is "no big deal."

Even if our minds are convinced that sex is no big deal, our souls know better. *Cosmopolitan* magazine sells millions of copies each month with tantalizing topics teaching women how to attract men. But what *Cosmo* and other similar magazines fail to teach a woman is what to do with her soul once it has been damaged. They don't offer much hope for the hurting or for the depressed, because they are too busy making billions by telling women that sex is "no big deal."

Lie #4: "I Will Feel More Secure If . . ."

This lie strikes at the desire in a woman's heart for emotional security. One area of weakness for women is to find our identity in feeling sexually attractive to men. While the longing to be found beautiful is innate to women, the twisting of this desire for beauty is something that Satan utilizes to his advantage. Countless women confessed to me that the more insecure they felt about their appearance, the more likely they were to give in to pressure or temptation. One woman candidly wrote:

> The times I have felt a strong temptation toward sexual sin, since I've been a Christian, have all been tied to my insecurities, mostly about how I look. When I am feeling unhappy with my body, I hear a faint whisper say, "There are definitely men out there who find you attractive and beautiful. It can't be too hard to find them." This thought would lead to the idea that if I hooked up with a guy, that experience would put my insecurities to rest because it would be proof that I'm still desirable.
>
> —age 32

Notice how she used the term *proof* that she was desirable. This lie tells women that a man's sexual desire for her is evidence of her value. It is easy to see how our Enemy sets us up, women especially, to believe this lie. We are bombarded with messages that tell us our worth is found in our beauty. In television and film, women are depicted as using their sexuality as a powerful tool to gain security. Yet this proves a dangerous double-edged sword, for one must continually work to be found beautiful or sexy in order to feel confident or secure.

As a result, insecurity can lead a woman to fall into temptation. If she believes the lie that a man's attention and desire equal her worth as a woman, then she will sacrifice her purity in an effort to fix her gaping hole of insecurity. This is the classic bait and switch. Not only does our Enemy fuel the media that brainwashes women to see themselves as sexual objects, but he also targets our insecurities so that we will use our bodies as a means to "feel secure."

I personally experienced the wickedness of this lie. While dating my husband, I went through some health issues, which caused me to gain a few pounds. Nothing drastic, but my normal clothing size did not fit anymore. Any woman reading this can understand how the weight gain could bring on bouts of insecurity about my appearance. Like any American girl, I, too, was brainwashed since birth to link my worth as a woman with my weight.

As weeks went by and the scale did not budge, I noticed an increase in temptation. The temptation whispered, *You will feel more secure if he desires you physically.* Just as with Eve, Satan promised me confidence, security, and value if I would just ignore God's Word. Through prayer and accountability, as well as by renewing my mind with truth, I was able to recognize the lie and stand against it.

This lie is so effective because there is a kernel of truth involved. The truth is that men do have a physical desire for sex. A woman's insecurity latches on to a man's innate desire and equates her ability to entice him with her personal value. This equation adds up to increasing insecurity and misplaced identity. A cherished woman is not bait to lure; she is a beauty to behold.

Lie #5: "He Will Love Me More If I Have Sex With Him"

I wanted the boy to love me so badly because he was the guy all the girls wanted to date, but he picked me. So once I had him, I did whatever he wanted. Even though I knew sex outside of marriage was not God's best for us, I believed the lie that he wouldn't really love me unless our relationship was sexual. Of course, now that he is history, I realize how stupid I was.

—age 17

When I desired to honor God with my body and walk in purity, I often heard, "Your boyfriend will love you more if you have sex with him."

—age 34

My boyfriend was sexually active before he began following Jesus. So when we started dating, temptation whispered in my ear, "He's already had sex with so many other women. How could he ever love you as much if you don't do that with him, as well?" I actually pressured him into sex because I was so insecure about the girls from his past.

—age 24

I often ask young women, "Are you buying the lie or believing the truth?" One of the most pervasive lies women believe is that sex is a commodity that can be traded for love. This lie is absolutely ingrained in our culture. Girls from great families or women from broken pasts—it really doesn't make much of a difference—have believed the lie that sex will secure the love they crave.

The human heart hungers for intimacy. We long to be known. The Bible often uses "to know" when speaking of the sexual relationship between husband and wife. "Adam *knew* Eve his wife, and she conceived and bore Cain" (Genesis 4:1 ESV, emphasis added). The knowledge that a husband and wife have of each other is expressed through sex, but sex is not the door to intimacy.

Genital sex is an expression of intimacy, not the means to intimacy. True intimacy springs from verbal and emotional communion. True intimacy is built on a commitment to honesty, love and freedom. True intimacy is not primarily a sexual encounter. Intimacy, in fact, has almost nothing to do with our sex organs. A prostitute may expose her body, but her relationships are hardly intimate.[5]

God created us in His image. We are relational creatures. Our desire for intimacy is not wrong; it is good. But it is wrong for us to believe that sexual activity will fill the ache in our souls that longs to be known.

In his book *Soul Cravings*, Erwin Raphael McManus writes:

> Sex can be the most intimate and beautiful expression of love, but we are only lying to ourselves when we act as if sex is proof of love. Too many men demand sex as proof of love; too many women have given sex in hopes of love. We live in a world of users where we abuse each other to dull the pain of aloneness. We all long for intimacy, and physical contact can appear as intimacy, at least for a moment.[6]

The flat-out honest truth is that any man you really want to have as a husband will respect you more if you abstain. I know what you're thinking: *Every guy wants sex!* Guess what? You're right! Sure, there are those guys out there who won't be interested in a relationship with you if you aren't sexually active. But stop and think about it. Is that the type of man you truly desire? One who is merely interested in your body and not your soul? Do you actually want to be with a man who refuses to cherish you?

Here is a promise you can take to the bank. Nothing is impossible with God. Girls, I prayed for many years for my godly husband, for a man who would lead our relationship in purity and who would cherish me. God provided that man!

I am beyond thankful for the hundreds of dateless Saturday nights that I endured. Not only did that time allow me to grow closer to Jesus, but God's best was very much worth waiting for. I wish I could convince every woman reading this that it is far better to remain single than to be with a man who doesn't cherish you. It is far better to lose a guy because you value purity rather than remain with a man who won't value you in the end.

There is also an empowering truth that I think some women fail to recognize. Sexual purity is not just about *you*. God calls both men and women to purity, but women are, for better or worse, the standard-bearers. We tend to set the boundaries in the relationship. You hold a God-given gift to call forth a man to maturity when you fight for sexual purity. In our culture of free sex, the men of our generation are not stepping up and making the mature decision to commit in order to satisfy their natural desires. When sexual favors are free, men don't feel the need to commit to a woman or cherish her.

God wired men to love a challenge. They are far more interested in a girl who makes them wait and fight for her affection than for a girl who uses her body to gain his love. Frankly, we lose so much when we give in. Sexual purity is more than just God's best for your soul. Purity is the pathway to your heart's desire to be loved, honored, and cherished.

Lie #6: "Everything Except Intercourse Is Fair Game"

When I was a new Christian, I met a guy on a mission trip. Our relationship started out innocent enough at first, but then one night he stayed over at my house, which led to him staying over every night. We messed around physically, and I justified it by thinking, *Oh, it's fine. We're not having sex.* I assumed that since we weren't having intercourse, we weren't sinning. Although we were not pure and we weren't honoring God, I would justify his spending the night by comparing it with my other friends' sins and think, *At least we're not having "sex."* Our physical relationship progressed little by little, and I didn't see anything wrong with any of it until we crossed the line. I justified the sin by comparing it with what I perceived to be "bigger" sins.

—Anonymous

The term *technical virginity* has been used to describe a person who thinks she is still a virgin as long as she hasn't had intercourse. She thinks that anything up to the point of penetration doesn't count. She has engaged in sexual activity (hooking up, sleepovers, oral sex, mutual masturbation, etc.), yet has not engaged in intercourse. She believes her actions are not immoral because "technically" sex did not occur.

In the church, this is by far one of Satan's greatest deceptions. He likes to deceive us into believing we've found a loophole that will keep us "pure" while still indulging our flesh. Not only does this lie damage us body, soul, and spirit, but it also leads us down a path of immorality and far from God's blessings.

Any woman committed to sexual purity must be on guard against this particular lie. Here is the truth: *Intercourse* is "physical contact between individuals that involves genitalia of at least one person."[7] Please note, it does not say *penetration*. It says "physical contact of genitalia." I must be blunt: The definition of intercourse includes oral sex, anal sex, mutual masturbation, fingering, rubbing, and grinding. (That was perhaps the most awkward sentence I've ever written in my entire life! But I can't hold back from speaking the truth.) Satan loves for us to think we are "pure" because we aren't "going all the way," even though we are practicing sin that God considers sexual immorality.

The Bible is clear when it comes to sexual immorality:

> Or do you not know that wrongdoers will not inherit the kingdom of God? Do not be deceived: Neither the sexually immoral nor idolaters nor adulterers nor men who have sex with men nor thieves nor the greedy nor drunkards nor slanderers nor swindlers will inherit the kingdom of God.
>
> 1 Corinthians 6:9–10

> Among you there must not be even a hint of sexual immorality, or of any kind of impurity, or of greed, because these are improper for God's holy people.
>
> Ephesians 5:3

God doesn't mess around when it comes to sex. (No pun intended.) Why? Because we are too precious in His eyes. He knows that sexual activity outside of marriage is a slippery slope to destruction. A little lust never satisfies. Our flesh will crave more and more. We must guard against thought patterns that lead us into sin.

Our heavenly Father longs for us to be cherished. He knows that when we give away sexual favors, we cheapen ourselves in the eyes of men. Engaging in sexual immorality prior to marriage not only degrades us but robs our future marriage of intimacy. Ladies, I will be frank. A woman is not cherished who is engaging in oral sex with a man who is not her husband. This is a far cry from being a treasure. Sexual activity (of all forms) outside of marriage is a sin against God and against our own bodies. Satan does not want you to know this or believe it. Be on guard of anything that seems like a loophole around God's commandment. Satan would rather lie to you with his false promises so that he can ultimately deceive you.

Lie #7: "I'm Not a Virgin, So It's Too Late for Me to Walk in Purity"

I thought it was okay to have sex with all these guys because I could never get my virginity back.

—age 16

Once I crossed the line I had set up as too far, I felt like I had failed and that I couldn't ever be redeemed. I thought I'd ruined myself, so I might as well go all the way.

—age 26

After my boyfriend and I broke up, I didn't really have any physical boundaries for myself anymore. I thought since I did everything with one guy I might as well do anything with another one. Most of the times it was fun in the moment, but even the times when I wanted to say no I couldn't. Every morning was the same. I would wake up in a haze with a nasty hangover and feel horrible about what I had done. I really wanted to have boundaries with guys, but I feared that they wouldn't like me if I told them no.

—age 23

After my divorce, I started dating. Although I was a virgin when I married, and I knew sex was designed for marriage, I constantly heard this whispering voice say, "You aren't a virgin anymore, so it doesn't really matter." Plus, if I wanted to get back in competition with all the single girls, I had to play the game.

—age 40

I'm going to be blunt . . . *again.* This particular lie makes my blood boil, for it is straight from the pit of hell. Satan specializes in deceiving us into believing that once we've sinned, we are beyond redemption. My heart breaks for the young women who hear any version of this lie because I've been there. Apathy cloaked in shame. I can't tell you the number of women who have shared with me that this one has haunted them more than any other. No sooner does the evil one tempt someone into sexual sin than he turns around and bombards her with lies of shame and defeat once she succumbs.

There is a sad misconception that if you lose your virginity, all is lost and you might as well continue down a path of sexual activity. Satan always wants us to believe we are beyond grace and beyond hope. This is a flat-out lie because it is never too late to obey God and walk in purity. God's best is always worth waiting for, and we can walk the narrow road that leads to life even if we have detoured in the past.

When I was nineteen years old, I gave my virginity to a guy I thought I loved. When he broke up with me to pursue another girl on campus, I was crushed. Each lie listed above was one that

I, too, believed. I thought sex would bring me love. I hoped we would be together forever. I thought I would feel more secure if he was sexually attracted to me. But then, when it was all over and I was left with a soul bonded to a man who wasn't around, I began to hear Satan's other lies. Whispers that said, "Why bother? Your purity is gone and there is no turning back."

I must stop here and say a word to any woman who has heard this one. Satan is a liar! Remember, Jesus said that Satan is the Father of Lies. The truth is that our God specializes in redemption. To redeem means to restore and return something to its original intent.

I can honestly say that I felt more pure on my wedding day than I did even before I technically lost my virginity. Purity is a life devoted to Christ. Jesus takes our mess, our insecurities, and our shame, and then He alone washes us clean and makes all things new! He robes us in His righteousness and restores us, body, mind, soul, and spirit. This is why I call myself a Redeemed Girl!

I say this to offer a word of hope and encouragement to anyone who is feeling shame or defeat. My purpose and prayer in exposing these lies is so that you can recognize and resist them. If you are currently struggling with any of these, take courage! God's grace is sufficient and His power is more than adequate to enable you to stand. I've heard each one of these lies personally, and I know how sinister and deceptive our Enemy can be. My ambition in exposing his deceptions is to equip you to resist him. Never forget, dear sister, greater is He (Jesus) who is in you than he who is in this world!

The Battleground

The primary battleground on which this war is waged is in your mind. The brain is command central for our entire body. Every action, every promise, every impulse originates from that vital organ.

But the mind is more than a mass of tissue and blood cradled in the cranium. Our thoughts have a spiritual component to them as well. It is a tremendous mistake to attempt to separate the spiritual from the psychological and physical components of life.[8]

—Robert Jeffress

My primary objective in exposing the seven common lies is so that you will be equipped to resist them. Cherished ones, repeat after me: We behave how we believe. If we believe Satan's lies, eventually that lie will bear fruit in our lives. As Robert Jeffress said, "The brain is command central for our entire body." This is the reason we stopped to examine these seven lies. Our thoughts hold great influence on our actions. For example . . .

A few years ago, I saw a film that illustrated the power a person's thoughts have to influence their behavior. *The Upside of Anger* depicts a middle-aged woman, a devoted wife and mother, who suspects her husband left her and moved to Paris with a younger woman. As the film unfolds, the audience watches as this woman's life falls apart because of this information. She feels hurt and rejected. The wound festers into an intense anger. In her rage she lashes out and pushes away friends and family. To deal with her loneliness and pain, she turns to alcohol, and her life is in shambles from the addiction.

At the conclusion of the movie, we discover that it is all a lie. Yes, a lie. Her husband did not cheat on her, nor did he leave her or move to Paris. Actually, he had tragically fallen into a pit behind their home and died. Everything the woman believed was a lie. And as a result, her feelings, emotions, and actions followed suit.

Our thoughts lead our emotions, and our emotions lead our actions. I'll say it again: We behave how we believe. Our thoughts have power. Therefore, as women of God, we must carefully inventory our thoughts and see if they align with the truth of God's Word. Bottom line, the battleground for purity is in our minds.

And this is great news. For the woman reading this who feels like she has fallen time and again in this arena, or for the woman reading this who wants to avoid a detour, victory is possible. Yes, there is a great war for our souls, but when we pinpoint Satan's access point in our minds, we can close the door to his assault.

Cherished ones, ask the Holy Spirit to reveal to you the specific lies you believe, the ones Satan uses to tempt you into sexual sin. Once you recognize these lies, you can begin to resist the evil one and stand in God's truth. I don't know about you, but I for one am sick and tired of seeing God's girls settle for so much less than God's best. Arise, sisters! It is time for the resistance of the cherished ones!

I gave him everything! I was half a virgin when I met him.

~ Regina George (Rachel McAdams)
in *Mean Girls*

9

The Resistance of the Cherished Ones

Be alert and of sober mind. Your enemy the devil prowls around like a roaring lion looking for someone to devour. Resist him.

1 Peter 5:8–9

As January 1 rolls around each year, most of us make New Year's resolutions. Studies show that by three weeks into the year, the resolutions are packed away with last year's Christmas décor.

It seems like each year I resolve to eat healthier and take better care of my body. Friends, let me just say, the spirit is willing but the flesh is weak! This year, I decided to banish gluten once and for all from my diet. According to my doctor, gluten is my kryptonite, and to eliminate it would make me a far healthier woman. Most of the time, I'm pretty good at saying no to bread, pizza, and the other major players. But do you realize how many delicious and delectable morsels include gluten? EVERYTHING CONTAINS GLUTEN! So by January 9, as I sat at a table with my favorite chocolate cake, I had a big decision: to give in and eat a piece, or resist the temptation?

The word *resist* implies a choice of our will. Our human will is the place of decision. When the temptation arises to choose God's way or to choose sin, we, with our human wills, can resist and say "no." Resisting the Enemy is choosing to believe in the moment of temptation that God is good and obedience is for our best.

The primary issue we face during temptation is Satan's craftiness. He hurls temptations that appeal directly to the desire of our sinful nature for pleasure, prominence, power, and prestige. He also entices us to meet legitimate needs in illegitimate ways (e.g., for the girl who desires love, she is tempted to use her body physically to achieve her desire). While this is a false intimacy and ultimately leads to destruction, Satan paints a beautifully alluring picture in her mind, tempting her with those thoughts that say, "Sex is no big deal" and, "He will love me if . . ." As Robert Jeffress so brilliantly observes, "The god of this world is constantly baiting us with the lie that only the things we don't yet possess will satisfy our deepest yearnings."[1]

Stop and think about your soul hunger. What rumbles inside of you that longs to be filled? Do you hunger for affection? Do you desire attention? Do you long to be known? Do you crave love? When these desires are unmet, the Enemy sees our vulnerability and seeks to detour us by tempting us to satisfy these longings in an illegitimate way. But we must beware! There is a trade-off.

The Trade-Off

The book of Genesis tells the story of two brothers, Jacob and Esau. Esau was the firstborn son who would one day inherit his father's estate. Not only was he the heir to worldly riches, but God also promised to this family that through their descendants, the entire world would be blessed (Genesis 12:1–3). This promise foretold the coming of Jesus Christ, the Messiah.

Esau was a man of destiny.

Esau was a man of privilege.

Esau was a man of purpose.

That is quite a future. Yet he traded it all. And for what? A bowl of stew.

> Once when Jacob was cooking some stew, Esau came in from the open country, famished. He said to Jacob, "Quick, let me have some of that red stew! I'm famished!" Jacob replied, "First sell me your birthright."
>
> "Look, I am about to die," Esau said. "What good is the birthright to me?" But Jacob said, "Swear to me first." So he swore an oath to him, selling his birthright to Jacob. Then Jacob gave Esau some bread and some lentil stew. He ate and drank, and then got up and left. So Esau despised his birthright.
>
> Genesis 25:29–34

Famished. Ravenous. Hungry. Empty . . . All Esau could think about was food. He was mad with hunger. And in this place of desperation, he traded it all—his birthright, fortune, name, and blessing. Esau gave it all to his brother, Jacob, for one measly bowl of stew.

This is also how sexual temptation works. When we are hungry—be that for love, affection, attention, affirmation, comfort, or belonging—temptation strikes. Cherished ones, I hope you will stop right now and take an honest look at your soul hunger. Don't sell your birthright as a cherished daughter of the King. A woman's fight for purity will always be a tough one if she is famished for affection. Dealing with these deeper issues is the key to victory.

A few years ago, I struggled a great deal with my singleness. Most of my close friends were married and I was still alone. Sure, my life was full and I was in love with Jesus, but I could not deny my soul hunger for love. Around that time, I started dating a man and fell in love with him. Even though he was a Christian, deep inside I knew we were not God's best for each other. But for months I pushed aside this knowledge and held on. I hoped we would marry, but that relationship eventually ended, leaving me heartbroken.

My pain was more than just the normal breakup blues. I was facing the reality that my longing for love and marriage would not be realized in that person. In the months following that breakup, I experienced the most intense battle for my mind that I've ever walked through in my entire life. I write of this battle in my book *Wilderness Skills for Women* (B&H, 2008).

Looking back on that season, I can see that the access point for the Enemy was my soul's deep hunger for love. Although I loved God and was serving Jesus, I was still operating out of a great deficiency. Unhealed wounds from my childhood caused a cavernous hole that I was hoping to fill with human love. These wounds, combined with my singleness and the disappointment of the breakup, left me wide open and vulnerable to Satan's schemes.

I share my experience with you because I know many of you reading this right now are in a similar position. You've waited. You're tired of being the bridesmaid. You've watched friend after friend find love, yet you still feel a gnawing pain. I get it. I've been there. And the honest truth is this: Every human being breathing air on this planet feels the same way. We all hunger for unfailing love.

Proverbs 19:22 speaks to this universal longing: "What is desirable in a man is his kindness, and it is better to be a poor man than a liar" (NASB). I love this verse. There is such freedom in these words. It's okay to own it and say, "I desire unfailing love."

Before I walked through my wilderness season of heartbreak and rejection, I thought the unfailing love I hungered for would be found in a person. I believed marriage was the answer to my heart's desire. But now I can honestly say that the best thing the Lord ever did for me was to allow my heart to be broken and for that relationship to end. You see, my heart was not safe. I, too, would have traded my destiny for a bowl of stew. Like Esau, my hunger screamed louder than common sense. God in His mercy stepped in so that I would not make such a disastrous decision.

God allowed my heart to be temporarily broken so that it would be permanently filled—not by a man, but by Him. What I needed more than a husband or any earthly love was for my heart to receive the unfailing love of God. My desire for acceptance, security, and belonging had to be first realized in Christ. The words of Oswald Chambers say it best: "No love of the natural heart is safe unless the human heart has been satisfied by God first."[2]

Today, on the other side of marriage, I know this to be a fact. I love my husband. He is wonderful to me, but the unfailing love my soul still craves must first be satisfied by Jesus. Only God can fill the God-spot. If I wrongly assume that Justin or any other human being can meet all of my emotional needs, I will be sorely disappointed.

Searching for perfect, unfailing love in anyone else is pointless. Jesus alone is the fount of Living Water that quenches the thirsty soul. Jesus alone is the Bread of Life that feeds the hungry heart. Our greatest desires are realized in Him.

John Piper said,

> Sin is what you do when your heart is not satisfied with God. No one sins out of duty. We sin because it holds out some promise of happiness. That promise enslaves us until we believe God is more to be desired than life itself.[3]

Think about it this way: Sexual sin occurs when a person attempts to satisfy a deep hunger for intimacy in an illegitimate way.

The Resistance

Now that we can recognize the lies and realize the vulnerability of our soul hunger, the question before us is this: How do we resist? Jesus' own experience provides one of the greatest examples of how we resist the Enemy in times of temptation. Matthew 4 tells of Jesus' journey into the wilderness, where He was tempted by the devil for forty days and nights: "Then Jesus was led by the Spirit into the wilderness to be tempted by the devil. After fasting forty days and forty nights, he was hungry" (vv. 1–2).

The opening verses hold the key to this narrative: Jesus was also tempted in the place of His hunger. While Jesus was hungry for food, notice what the Enemy did: "The tempter came to him and said, 'If you are the Son of God, tell these stones to become bread'" (v. 3).

Our Enemy does the same to us. When we are hungry for love, acceptance, importance, recognition, or anything the human heart can desire, he tempts us to satisfy this hunger in a way that is disobedient to our heavenly Father. Think back to those seven lies we uncovered in the previous chapter. Each one strikes at a place of hunger in a woman's heart—our hunger for love, security, comfort, belonging, or acceptance. Behind each lie is the Enemy enticing us to meet our legitimate need in an illegitimate way.

Thankfully, Jesus is not only our Savior; He is also our example, and He empowers us to resist Satan just as He did. Notice how Jesus withstood the temptation. He responded to each one of the devil's lies with the truth of God's Word. Jesus answered, "It is written: 'Man shall not live on bread alone, but on every word that comes from the mouth of God'" (v. 4).

Quoting from the Old Testament, Jesus used Scripture to battle Satan's temptation. The Word of God is powerful! The truth sends the liar running. When Satan speaks his deceptive lies, our weapon against his schemes is the sword of the Spirit, which Ephesians 6 tells us is the Word of God. While in the wilderness, Jesus faced three major temptations. Each time, He resisted Satan by speaking Scripture out loud—specifically countering each lie with truth. We can effectively resist temptation in the same way Jesus did.

In the midst of my own battle, the Lord reminded me of how He responded to Satan's schemes by saying, "Marian, pick up your sword. . . . It's time to fight." Cherished ones, our sword is the Word of God.

> Finally, be strong in the Lord and in his mighty power. Put on the full armor of God, so that you can take your stand against the devil's schemes. For our struggle is not against flesh and blood, but against the rulers, against the authorities, against the powers of this dark world and against the spiritual forces of evil in the heavenly realms. Therefore put on the full armor of God, so that when the day of evil comes, you may be able to stand your ground, and after you have done everything, to stand. Stand firm then, with the belt of truth buckled around your waist, with the breastplate of righteousness in place, and with your feet fitted with the readiness that comes from the gospel of peace. In addition to all this, take up the shield of faith, with which you can extinguish all the flaming arrows of the evil one. Take the helmet of salvation and the sword of the Spirit, which is the word of God.
>
> Ephesians 6:10–17

We must remember that God equipped us with spiritual armor to wear! He equipped us to resist and to withstand the evil one. Each piece of the armor is needed, but in our battle for sexual purity, one of the key weapons in our arsenal is the sword of the Spirit.

Notice that the sword of the Spirit is clearly defined as the Word of God. God breathed truth to us and for us. His Word proves powerful in refuting the lies of the Evil One. I should know. By wielding the sword of the Spirit, I was able to resist Satan's lies and win the battle for sexual purity. Here is what I did to resist.

Step 1: I bought a small ringed note-card holder. A journal will also work, or you can just as easily use a smartphone.

Step 2: I searched my Bible for every verse I could find on sexual purity or resisting temptation. Once I recognized the Enemy's lies, I knew I needed specific words of God to counteract his schemes. When I found a Scripture that spoke to my struggle, I wrote it on a card and meditated on it throughout the day. Using your phone, you could type Scriptures into Notes and review it throughout the day.

For example, I wrote on a note card Hebrews 13:4: "Marriage should be honored by all, and the marriage bed kept pure, for God will judge the adulterer and all the sexually immoral."

As I would drive the three hours between our cities (Justin and I dated long distance), I would recite God's truth over and over to myself. My battle verses renewed my mind and helped me to remember why we were choosing to fight. As Psalm 119:11 says, "I have hidden your word in my heart that I might not sin against you."

Shannon Ethridge, author of *Every Woman's Battle*, speaks to our power to choose our thoughts when she writes,

> Even though inappropriate thoughts inevitably pop up into every person's mind, we do not have to entertain them. Such thoughts are not sin, but dwelling on such thoughts is essential to rehearsing for rebellion, and acting on such thoughts is sin. We can't keep from being tempted, but we can avoid rehearsing, and we can certainly refuse to sin. No temptation becomes sin without our permission.[4]

Girls, did you hear that powerful truth? *No temptation becomes sin without our permission!* We have the power to choose what we do with our thoughts. Sure, Satan's lies and temptations will come, but we possess the power to choose whether or not we will dwell on or entertain those thoughts.

Step 3: When those thoughts and lies entered my mind, I would speak out loud, just as Jesus did, the Word of God. This is when we put into action the truth of Romans 12:2, which says, "Do not conform to the pattern of this world, but be transformed by the renewing of your mind." The Word of God proves powerful! As I meditated on God's truth, a marvelous transformation occurred. I found my will (the place of decision within a person) strengthened, and my desire aligned more with God's will. I desired to choose obedience, and the temptations became less alluring because I now recognized them as destructive detours. During specific moments of weakness, I would read the Scriptures out loud and sense a new power from the Spirit and a lessening of temptation's hold on my mind.

Ladies, trust me, our Enemy will flee, just as he did when Jesus rebuked him. We can demolish his lies with God's truth. My challenge to you is this: *If you are facing a battle, take up your sword.* Open your Bible. Discover what God's Word says about your struggle. Resist the Enemy! Here are just a few of the battle verses that I wrote in my personal Scripture journal. I pray these help you to resist the lies and stand in victory.

Battle Verses

The night is nearly over; the day is almost here. So let us put aside the deeds of darkness and put on the armor of light. Let us behave decently, as in the daytime, not in carousing and drunkenness, not in sexual immorality and debauchery, not in dissension and jealousy. Rather, clothe yourselves with the Lord Jesus Christ, and do not think about how to gratify the desires of the flesh.

Romans 13:12–14

Marriage should be honored by all, and the marriage bed kept pure, for God will judge the adulterer and all the sexually immoral.

Hebrews 13:4

Flee from sexual immorality. All other sins a person commits are outside the body, but whoever sins sexually, sins against their own body. Do you not know that your bodies are temples of the Holy Spirit, who is in you, whom you have received from God? You are not your own; you were bought at a price. Therefore honor God with your bodies.

1 Corinthians 6:18–20

Be alert and of sober mind. Your enemy the devil prowls around like a roaring lion looking for someone to devour. Resist him, standing firm in the faith, because you know that the family of believers throughout the world is undergoing the same kind of sufferings.

1 Peter 5:8–9

[Jesus said,] "Nevertheless, I have this against you: You tolerate that woman Jezebel, who calls herself a prophet. By her teaching she misleads my servants into sexual immorality and the eating of food sacrificed to idols. I have given her time to repent of her immorality, but she is unwilling. So I will cast her on a bed of suffering, and I will make those who commit adultery with her suffer intensely, unless they repent of her ways."

Revelation 2:20–22

So, if you think you are standing firm, be careful that you don't fall! No temptation has overtaken you except what is common to mankind. And God is faithful; he will not let you be tempted beyond what you can bear. But when you are tempted, he will also provide a way out so that you can endure it.

1 Corinthians 10:12–14

If they have escaped the corruption of the world by knowing our Lord and Savior Jesus Christ and are again entangled in it and are overcome, they are worse off at the end than they were at the beginning. It would have been better for them not to have known the way of righteousness, than to have known it and then to turn their backs on the sacred command that was passed on to them.

Of them the proverbs are true: "A dog returns to its vomit," and, "A sow that is washed returns to her wallowing in the mud."

2 Peter 2:20–22

Dear friends, I urge you, as foreigners and exiles, to abstain from sinful desires, which wage war against your soul. Live such good lives among the pagans that, though they accuse you of doing wrong, they may see your good deeds and glorify God on the day he visits us.

1 Peter 2:11–12

Don't you know that you yourselves are God's temple and that God's Spirit dwells in your midst?

1 Corinthians 3:16

Be very careful, then, how you live—not as unwise but as wise, making the most of every opportunity, because the days are evil. Therefore do not be foolish, but understand what the Lord's will is. Do not get drunk on wine, which leads to debauchery. Instead, be filled with the Spirit.

Ephesians 5:15–18

It is God's will that you should be sanctified: that you should avoid sexual immorality; that each of you should learn to control your own body in a way that is holy and honorable, not in passionate lust like the pagans, who do not know God; and that in this matter no one should wrong or take advantage of a brother or sister. The Lord will punish all those who commit such sins, as we told you and warned you before. For God did not call us to be impure, but to live a holy life. Therefore, anyone who rejects this instruction does not reject a human being but God, the very God who gives you his Holy Spirit.

1 Thessalonians 4:3–8

For though we live in the world, we do not wage war as the world does. The weapons we fight with are not the weapons of the world.

On the contrary, they have divine power to demolish strongholds. We demolish arguments and every pretension that sets itself up against the knowledge of God, and we take captive every thought to make it obedient to Christ.

2 Corinthians 10:3–5

His divine power has given us everything we need for a godly life through our knowledge of him who called us by his own glory and goodness. Through these he has given us his very great and precious promises, so that through them you may participate in the divine nature, having escaped the corruption in the world caused by evil desires.

2 Peter 1:3–4

Therefore do not let sin reign in your mortal body so that you obey its evil desires. Do not offer any part of yourself to sin as an instrument of wickedness, but rather offer yourselves to God as those who have been brought from death to life; and offer every part of yourself to him as an instrument of righteousness. For sin shall no longer be your master, because you are not under the law, but under grace.

Romans 6:12–14

Guys, a woman's purse, all right, it's her secret source of power. All right? There are many dark and dangerous things in there, that we, the male species, should know nothing about.

~ Ben Barry (Matthew McConaughey)
in *How to Lose a Guy in 10 Days*

10

Winning the Battle Within

Our reliance on the Spirit is not intended to foster an attitude of "I can't do it," but one of "I can do it through Him who strengthens me." The Christian should never complain of want of ability and power. If we sin, it is because we choose to sin, not because we lack the ability to say no to temptation.

—Jerry Bridges, *The Pursuit of Holiness*

Just this week I met another casualty in Satan's great war against the soul—a single Christian woman who has fallen in defeat time and time again. On the verge of hopelessness, she's beginning to feel like victory is impossible for her. She found me during the prayer time after my message and said, "I really need your help. I don't know what to do. I know what I'm supposed to do and not supposed to do, but I fail every time. Maybe I'm just not good at following Jesus."

Shame was written all over her, and I could feel her pain. She's looking at her sin record, and the enormity of her failure is just depressing. She's heard all the Scriptures about forgiveness, and after a while, they ring in her ears like clichés. She doesn't feel "white as snow" or like a "new creation." She feels like she keeps standing up and falling down . . . over and over again. After listening to her story and asking a few questions to confirm her salvation, I discerned her primary problem was this: She did not know how to win the battle within.

To explain the nature of the battle within, I need to stop and clarify some essential biblical theology. As Christ-followers, we are born again when we place faith in Jesus Christ. (See John 3:3–15.) The Word of God says we become new creations in Christ (2 Corinthians 5:17). This is amazing! In God's great love story, He awakens us into new life with Him. At the point of our spiritual new birth, the Holy Spirit resides with us. As 1 Corinthians 3:16 says, "Do you not know that you are a *temple of God* and that the Spirit *of God* dwells in you?" (NASB, emphasis added). Now we are the temple of God. Cherished one, you are holy ground. This is called the indwelling of the Spirit.

Once we are born again, we now have two natures: We have our new nature, which is the Spirit of God who indwells us, but we also have our old nature, which is our sinful nature (also called the flesh). These two natures are at war. They have opposing agendas, which the apostle Paul clearly describes.

> So I say, walk by the Spirit, and you will not gratify the desires of the flesh. For the flesh desires what is contrary to the Spirit, and the Spirit what is contrary to the flesh. They are in conflict with each other, so that you are not to do whatever you want.
>
> Galatians 5:16–17

The Holy Spirit wants us to obey God and live a holy life in order to glorify Jesus. For this reason, when we are born again, we do have new desires. The Holy Spirit births into our hearts a love for God, and the Spirit convicts us if our actions are outside of God's will. I recall after I surrendered my life to Jesus, I could not go to the same places and practice the same activities I had engaged in before Christ. I felt conviction and remorse. This was evidence of the new nature—the Holy Spirit of God at work.

But there is still a war raging within every believer. We still have our old, sinful nature that we must deal with. The flesh huffs and puffs and says, "Not so fast. . . . I want to do what I want to do!" For a Christian, it is our flesh that chooses sexual sin. As Paul says in Galatians, "The acts of the flesh are obvious: sexual immorality, impurity and debauchery" (5:19).

The young woman I met with the other night was a Christian; she was born again. But her problem was the same as many—she was still allowing her flesh to dominate and control her. In the great tug-of-war for her will, the flesh was winning. Although she's known Jesus as Savior since she was a young girl, she never learned how to *live by the Spirit*.

Sitting her down, I tried to comfort her and give her hope that victory is possible, but she would need to make some changes and apply truth to her thinking. I began by assuring her that winning the battle for sexual purity was *not* ever going to happen in her own strength. Yes, you read that correctly: PURITY IS NOT POSSIBLE IN HUMAN STRENGTH! None of us, apart from God's Spirit, can live a holy life. After all, this is why Jesus came to die for us. Right? We are sinners who need a Savior.

The incredible truth that many Christians fail to recognize is this: There is more to the Gospel than just salvation. Through the power of the Holy Spirit, we can live in victory. Most people have tried and failed to live sexually pure lives by simply following rules or by their own willpower. Neither of these methods will work. We must have Holy Spirit power! Get this. The same Spirit who raised Jesus from the dead lives in you! (Romans 8:11). Try to wrap your mind around that one. He is our power source to live a holy life. Apart from Him, we can't do it.

Grasping my new friend's hand, I told her that she must begin to feed the spirit within her so that her new nature would grow stronger and her old, sinful nature would grow weaker. I sensed she was a little confused at this, so I turned to one of the best explanations I've ever heard on this topic.

Taking a deep breath, I said, "Imagine we have two puppy dogs. Let's name one puppy flesh and the other, spirit. Now, what would happen if we fed one every day, but we never fed the other?" Shrugging her shoulders, she said, "I guess he would stop growing or die."

Excited that she was grasping the truth, I said, "Exactly! That's precisely what happens to us. As we go through life, we are either feeding our flesh or we are feeding our spirit. When we feed our flesh, our old, sinful nature grows stronger and stronger, and resisting it proves harder and harder. But when we feed our spirit, God's power within us grows, and it is easier to resist temptations and walk in victory."

Her eyes lit up and a big smile spread across her face. For the first time, her history of continual defeats made sense. She finally had hope that she could live a life of sexual purity. Her next question absolutely made my day. "So how do I starve the flesh and feed my spirit?" The Bible teacher in me wanted to pick her up, spin her around, and do a little dance. But since I knew she had mustered up all the courage she had just to talk to me about her struggle, I thought it best to just give her a little side hug. So I did. (But deep inside I was dancing!)

I think her question is one that many Christian women are afraid to ask. We desire to honor God, but we often find ourselves falling into temptations and wondering, *What happened?*

To feed our spirit, we must learn to abide in Christ daily. The Holy Spirit is our power source to live a pure life. His power increases in us the more we remain connected to Jesus and yield to His influence.

Abide

If you are anything like me, you love Jesus and desire to live for His glory, but there are times when you, too, feel like an absolute spiritual failure. You think Britney Spears' hit "Oops, I Did It Again" was written just for you. On top of that, you may feel completely exhausted from trying hard to be a "good Christian girl." I have good news for you. This is not how God intended the Christian life to be lived.

The Christian life is not "try harder" and "do better." The victorious Christian life is reliance on the Holy Spirit of God. When we aren't living by the power of the Spirit, we are striving and failing, striving and failing. This leads to what some people call spiritual burnout. I've come to learn that these feelings are evidence that I am attempting to live the Christian life out of my own strength. All too quickly, I discover that my ability to love, to forgive, to speak truth, and to live a holy life runs out before my morning coffee even gets cold. In these moments, Jesus sweetly reminds my striving heart, "Apart from me, you can do nothing." What a relief it is to remember that Jesus never expected me to be perfect without Him or to "experience the abundant life" apart from His Spirit. This is why the secret to the Christian life is abiding in Christ, which also proves to be our power to win the battle for sexual purity.

The Bible is filled with tangible, ordinary, real-life illustrations to help us understand deeply profound spiritual concepts. In order to illustrate our dependency on God, Jesus used an everyday example from nature—the relationship between a vine and a branch.

> "I am the true vine, and My Father is the vinedresser. Every branch in Me that does not bear fruit, He takes away; and every branch that bears fruit, He prunes it so that it may bear more fruit. You are already clean because of the word which I have spoken to you. Abide in Me, and I in you. As the branch cannot bear fruit of itself unless it abides in the vine, so neither can you unless you abide in Me. I am the vine, you are the branches; he who abides in Me and I in him, he bears much fruit, for apart from Me you can do nothing."
>
> John 15:1–5 NASB

Abide means to fully rely on or remain connected to Jesus. So how do we abide in Christ? We now know that *abide* means to stay connected to Jesus, but in this crazy, caffeine-induced, fast-paced, Twitter-fed, Instagram world that we call normal life, how do we slow down and remain connected to Jesus? The following acronym is how I've learned to D.A.I.L.Y. abide in Christ: Dedicate, Ask, Invite, Love, Yield.

D . . . Dedicate

First, we must **dedicate time** each day to spending with God. A relationship with Jesus is like any other relationship in that it requires communication. Through prayer we speak to God, and when we open God's Word, He speaks to us. I find the mornings, before the hustle and bustle of the day, to be the best for spending time with the Lord. When I start my day with Jesus, I am more sensitive to His voice leading me and speaking to me throughout the day.

There are many devotional books and quiet-time guides available, but I recommend reading a portion of Scripture each day, following a Bible-through-the-year plan. There are ample apps and free online resources to help you with this, and the payoff is huge. (See my website, www.redeemedgirl.org, for a daily Bible reading plan.) When I begin my day in God's Word, His truth fortifies me for the moments of temptation. I can more easily recognize Satan's lies because I've been soaking in the truth.

A . . . Ask

During my daily quiet time, I **ask** Jesus to fill me with His Holy Spirit. This is a time of confessing my weaknesses and asking God to give me His strength. This prayer is twofold. First, I lay down my sin and struggles with my palms facing down. Then, as I ask God to fill me, I turn my palms upward and invite the Holy Spirit to empower me. This is not a magic formula, but I feel connected to the prayer when I add the physical movements to the requests.

Sexual purity is one aspect of this empowering. While dating my husband, I would confess to God my weaknesses: my soul hunger for love, the lies that hounded my insecurities, and the various temptations. I would bring those thoughts and struggles to Christ. On my knees before God, I would lay those issues down. Then I would open up my palms and ask God to fill me with His Spirit. I would specifically ask for the strength to resist temptation. I would specifically ask for wisdom. I would specifically ask for His Spirit to increase in me so that I could say no to my flesh.

I . . . Invite

The next key to abiding in Christ daily is to **invite** the Holy Spirit into specific life circumstances throughout your day. We all face situations that tempt our flesh to sin. Our relationship with

God does not end at the conclusion of our morning quiet time. The wonderful truth is that God is *with* us and *in* us every step of the way. His power and strength are always ours, if and when we choose to rely upon Him.

For example, when Justin and I were dating, there were times that we would arrive at my house, expecting my roommates to be home. But to our surprise, we were alone. (TROUBLE!) Before getting out of the car to go inside, we would stop and pray. We simply invited the Lord to be present with us, to guard us from temptation, and to empower us to resist. Inviting the Holy Spirit to empower us in each moment proved to be a powerful way to resist our Enemy.

L . . . Love

As we abide in Christ each day, we must keep in mind that we are in a relationship with Him. The basis of this relationship is **love**. Jesus said the greatest commandment is *to love God and to love others*. As we walk with Jesus each day, we consciously make choices that reflect our love for Him. This is crucial in our battle for sexual purity. As I've said in previous chapters, rules will be broken, but a vision will be lived. When our hearts love God, and His glory is our ambition, then we desire to obey Him. Love always motivates obedience.

The secret to abiding in Christ is to let love be your guide. Throughout my many years of singleness, this truth informed most of my dating choices.

Will this guy cause me to love Jesus more or less?

Would this activity reflect to the world that I love Jesus?

Does this relationship lead me closer to Jesus or further away?

As I said in chapter 1, in the height of our engagement bliss, the greatest thing that kept us pure was our mutual love for the Lord. At the end of a date, we would look at each other and say, "I love you, but I love Jesus more. Therefore, I'm going home."

Jesus said in John 14:15, "If you love me, keep my commands." When daily abiding in Christ, a woman's love for God is what propels her to choose purity.

Y . . . Yield

The final step in daily abiding in Christ is **yielding to the Spirit of God.** Another word for *yield* is *surrender.* This occurs when our heart's response to the Lord is "not my will, but Thy will be done." The Holy Spirit always wants to glorify Jesus, and when we surrender to Him—instead of to our sinful nature—He leads us in ways that honor God.

Each day should begin by kneeling before God in our quiet time and yielding control to Him. This is done through prayer, but it's also done moment by moment when we face temptation. Think about it this way: When temptation strikes, there is a split-second decision made—we either yield to the flesh and sin or yield to the Holy Spirit and obey. Jerry Bridges wisely said, "Every time we say yes to temptation, we make it harder to say no the next time."[1] The opposite is true, as well. Each time we surrender to the Holy Spirit and say yes to obedience, the easier it is the next time we face a similar temptation.

Help!

In my walk with Jesus, I've found the single best prayer I have ever prayed is one word: "Help!" This is the word I uttered when I was sitting in a bar and came face-to-face with the emptiness of my life without God. This is the prayer I prayed after surrendering my life to Christ and realizing I needed Christian friends. "Help" was my plea when I went through a heartbreak and didn't think I could get out of bed and put my feet to the floor.

One. Simple. Powerful. Word . . .

"Help!"

Have you ever heard the statement "It takes one to know one"? I experienced this cliché this morning when I checked my email and discovered a sister in Christ asking for help.

She'd detoured.

Today she feels stuck, but she desperately wants to change. She wants to walk in purity, but she's being honest . . . she doesn't know *how*. Sure, she loves God, but over and over again, her relationships turn sexual. Each time she hopes it will turn out differently—love, marriage . . . happily ever after—but it doesn't. She confessed, "I want purity. I want to honor God, but I don't know how to change." She needs . . . *help*.

It takes one to know one.

I easily recognize her desperation, because I've been there. I remember when I first trusted Jesus, the shocking reality of how little I could trust myself emerged. I knew then, as I know now, that my flesh could not be trusted! I was scared. Scared because I didn't want to detour again but didn't trust myself not to do it.

Does anyone out there reading this know what I mean?

Back then I realized that if sexual purity were up to me, I was going to fail—big time! Thankfully, that one big, powerful prayer, "Help," proved reliable again. Girls, check this out . . . God never expected us to live the abundant Christian life by our own power. This is why He gave us the Holy Spirit—"the Helper." Jesus said, "the Helper, the Holy Spirit, whom the Father will send in My name, He will teach you all things" (John 14:26 NASB). You are not fighting a losing battle! The power of God resides in you!

Check out what the Bible says in Romans concerning our power source.

You, however, are not in the realm of the flesh but are in the realm of the Spirit, if indeed the Spirit of God lives in you. And if anyone does not have the Spirit of Christ, they do not belong to Christ. But if Christ is in you, then even though your body is subject to death because of sin, the Spirit gives life because of righteousness. And if the Spirit of him who raised Jesus from the dead is living in you, he who raised Christ from the dead will also give life to your mortal bodies because of his Spirit who lives in you.

Romans 8:9–11

Stop. Think about this truth: The same Spirit who raised Jesus from the dead lives in you! He is your Helper. Whether you are fighting temptation or struggling with insecurity, ask for His power to resist and overcome. He will empower you if you call upon Him.

Trust me, sisters. I am a living, breathing testimony to this power. With my sinful past and my brokenness, I thought sexual purity was impossible. But with God all things are possible!

P.U.R.E.

Some of you reading this right now are in the midst of sexual sin and need immediate help. Others of you have walked away from sexual sin in your past, but you still don't feel "pure." Good news! The Spirit of the living God is with you to restore and to renew you. I created the acronym P.U.R.E. to help women understand how the Holy Spirit renews our purity: Pray, Untangle, Renew, Exit.

Pray:

When King David was entangled in sexual sin, he prayed, "Create in me a pure heart, O God, and renew a steadfast spirit within me" (Psalm 51:10). This plea for renewal is a prayer of repentance. *Repentance* means to change. John MacArthur said, "Repentance is not just a change of mind; it is a change of heart.

It is a spiritual turning, a total about-face."[2] Repentance begins by coming before God in honest confession. Tell Jesus your sin. *After all, He already knows everything.* There is a flat-out supernatural power in confession. Don't look for loopholes and don't compare your purity to others. God's holiness is our standard, and His Word encourages us to confess: "If we confess our sins, he is faithful and just and will forgive us our sins and purify us from all unrighteousness" (1 John 1:9).

After I became a follower of Jesus Christ, I was blessed with an amazing woman of God who mentored me. My friend and mentor was the safe person I confessed my past sexual sin to. Together we prayed, asking God to cleanse me from my past. The Bible says in James 5:16, "Confess your sins to each other . . . so that you may be healed." I know my healing from the sexual sin of my past was due in large part to the specific times of confession and prayer with my mentor.

The big first step for a woman who desires sexual purity is prayer. Seek out a trusted friend or mentor who loves God and ask her to pray with you. There is a supernatural power in this prayer.

The old hymn is called "Amazing Grace" for a reason. When we recognize the power of God's grace to transform us, we stand in awe of His mercy. As we confess our sin, He washes over us with an outpouring of mercy and grace. Not only does God cleanse us from our past sin, but He lavishly forgives us. The Bible says He makes us white as snow.

- forgiven
- clean
- whole
- pure

Confession is life-changing. Don't shrink back. Run boldly to the throne of Grace—because His grace truly is amazing!

Untangle:

As we learned in previous chapters, soul ties form when two people are sexually involved. But in order to walk in purity, we must untangle ourselves from sinful relationships. This could mean ending a dating relationship or breaking off a friendship that is unhealthy. The Bible says to "lay aside every encumbrance and the sin which so easily entangles us, and let us run with endurance the race that is set before us" (Hebrews 12:1 NASB).

How do we do this? Begin by immediately ending any sexual relationship. Hear me, dear sister. Satan does not want you to do this. He wants you to remain entangled in sin. He will suggest every reason under the sun why you shouldn't. Don't listen to the Father of Lies. God's Word tells us to "lay aside every sin which entangles us."

Enlist a godly friend or pastor to pray for you. Ask for accountability to help you stand firm and to pray for you when you are tempted to text that guy or want to see him again. (In the next chapter, we will discuss the importance of accountability.) Breaking off a sexual relationship is not easy, but I promise you this: God will bless your obedience. In moments of weakness, specifically ask the Holy Spirit to fill you with strength and self-control, which is, by the way, a fruit of the Spirit (Galatians 5:22–24).

The following is a sample prayer for breaking soul ties that have occurred from sexual relationships. I recommend praying this prayer for each person with whom you were sexually involved. (Once again, we are defining sex as more than just intercourse.)

Dear Heavenly Father,

As your child, I come to you based on the forgiveness found in Jesus Christ. Through your Son, I am forgiven and redeemed. Jesus, I believe that you have taken away my guilt and shame at the cross. I believe your blood is powerful to cleanse me from my sin.

*Father, I ask in Jesus' Holy name that you break any soul
tie that exists between me and _____.*

*I confess our relationship was sinful. I confess I broke
your holy commandments. I believe that I am forgiven because of Jesus, and now I ask that you release any hold
that relationship or sexual experience still has on my life. I
want to be free from this person and my past. I ask that you
separate me body, mind, soul, and spirit from _____.
Holy Spirit, please cleanse me, renew me, and restore me.
I pray for my heart and mind to be free from any tie in the
spiritual realm to _____.*

*Holy Father, I thank you that you hear my prayer. I thank
you that your Son, Jesus, came to set the captives free! I
thank you that you are my Healer and my Deliverer. I thank
you that you have broken this tie and that I am free.*

*In the Holy name of Jesus,
Amen*

Renew:

In previous chapters we learned how the battlefield is our mind
and how the Enemy lies to lead us into sin. Therefore, the next
step in restoring purity is for a woman to immerse herself in God's
Word. When we do so, the Holy Spirit renews our minds. The
word *renew* means to renovate, revamp, or restore. God literally
changes *how* we think as we spend time in His Word.

Do not conform to the pattern of this world, but be transformed
by the renewing of your mind. Then you will be able to test and
approve what God's will is—his good, pleasing and perfect will.

Romans 12:2

For though we live in the world, we do not wage war as the world
does. The weapons we fight with are not the weapons of the world.

On the contrary, they have divine power to demolish strongholds. We demolish arguments and every pretension that sets itself up against the knowledge of God, and we take captive every thought to make it obedient to Christ.

2 Corinthians 10:3–5

How can a young person stay on the path of purity? By living according to your word.

Psalm 119:9

After I surrendered my life to Jesus, I began devouring Bible studies. My hunger for truth increased every day. I had a voracious appetite to study God's Word—the more I studied Scripture, the more I craved it. And here's the supernatural truth . . . the payoff was a pure mind!

Before Christ, as a single woman living in a culture that says sex is no big deal, my thoughts were conformed to the culture around me. But after immersing my mind in Scripture, I truly became a new creation. I began to think about and see sex and purity differently. Rather than agreeing with the world, I began to agree with God and viewed sex as sacred and purity as worth fighting for.

Purity was not just a change of external behaviors; God's Word literally scrubbed my mind clean, restored my innocence, and made me "new" from the inside out (Ephesians 5:26). For any woman who desires to remain sexually pure, she must commit herself to spending time in God's Word on a daily basis so that our thoughts are conformed to His truth rather than the lies and deceptions of the world.

Exit:

The final step in renewing purity is to establish an *exit* strategy. We will discuss in the next chapter the importance of not putting ourselves into situations where we will be easily tempted, but sometimes temptation finds us when we least expect it. In these moments, the Bible tells us what to do:

> Flee from sexual immorality. All other sins a person commits are outside the body, but whoever sins sexually, sins against their own body.
>
> 1 Corinthians 6:18

> No temptation has overtaken you except what is common to mankind. And God is faithful; he will not let you be tempted beyond what you can bear. But when you are tempted, he will also provide a way out so that you can endure it.
>
> 1 Corinthians 10:13

Cherished one, I hope and pray you grasp this powerful truth: God has endowed you with His Spirit for victory! He is our "exit" out of sin. The Holy Spirit who indwells us is your Helper. He will help you "flee" from the temptation. Just admit your weakness and rely upon Him for strength. When struggling with a big temptation, just say, "Help!" The Word promises that He will provide you a way out.

You're the first boy I ever kissed, Jake, and I want you to be the last.

~ Melanie Carmichael/Smooter (Reese Witherspoon)
in *Sweet Home Alabama*

11

The Wise Woman Wins the War

Wisdom is the right use of knowledge.

—Charles Spurgeon

Wisdom

Whether you are fifteen or fifty, it is hard not to love Taylor Swift. For many of us, she's a guilty pleasure. During the darkest days of post-breakups, I'd listen to her music and think, *At least one person out there understands how I feel.* And then, when blissfully falling in love with my husband, I'd turn up T-Swift in the car and sing "Love Story" at the top of my lungs. Don't judge. I'm not ashamed.

I think women of all ages can relate to her songs because she's not afraid to let her girl-flag fly. She expresses the emotions that we all feel but are too afraid to say out loud. One of the things she does best in her songs is admit that sometimes women don't make the smartest choices. With the perspective of time, we can look back and see how foolishness played into our decision making. In an interview, Miss Swift said:

> When I was a little girl I used to read fairy tales. In fairy tales you meet Prince Charming and he's everything you ever wanted. In fairy tales the bad guy is very easy to spot. The bad guy is always wearing a black cape so you always know who he is. Then you grow up and you realize that Prince Charming is not as easy to find as you thought. You realize the bad guy is not wearing a black cape and he's not easy to spot; he's really funny, and he makes you laugh, and he has perfect hair.[1]

If you are anything like me, you, too, can reflect on times that you didn't make the wisest choices, thinking to yourself:

How could I have been such a fool?

I should have seen that one coming!

But . . . I knew better!

And the worst thought of all . . . wait for it . . .

Oh dear . . . MY MOTHER WAS RIGHT!

Foolish choices are the ones we regret . . . BIG TIME! They tend to lead us down a path of heartbreak . . . not to mention embarrassment. But then we turn around and beat ourselves up for our foolishness. Thankfully, we don't have to live in a cycle of *wash-rinse-repeat* when it comes to foolish choices. God equips us with wisdom to make smart choices that lead to godly blessings. For this reason, Ephesians 5:15–17 advises us:

> Be very careful, then, how you live—not as unwise but as wise, making the most of every opportunity, because the days are evil. Therefore do not be foolish, but understand what the Lord's will is.

A wise woman not only knows what she should do or not do, she acts upon it. Wisdom is more than just knowledge. A person can acquire much knowledge and lack wisdom. Wisdom is the soundness of an action or decision with regard to the application of such experience, knowledge, and good judgment. Jerry Bridges, in his book *The Practice of Godliness*, describes wisdom as "an understanding and application of the moral principles of God."[2] Hear how Proverbs speaks of wisdom:

> My son, if you accept my words and store up my commands within you, turning your ear to wisdom and applying your heart to understanding—indeed, if you call out for insight and cry aloud for understanding, and if you look for it as for silver and search for it as for hidden treasure, then you will understand the fear of the Lord and find the knowledge of God.
>
> For the Lord gives wisdom; from his mouth come knowledge and understanding. He holds success in store for the upright, he is a shield to those whose walk is blameless, for he guards the course of the just and protects the way of his faithful ones. Then you will understand what is right and just and fair—every good path.
>
> For wisdom will enter your heart, and knowledge will be pleasant to your soul. Discretion will protect you, and understanding will guard you. Wisdom will save you from the ways of wicked men, from men whose words are perverse, who have left the straight paths to walk in dark ways, who delight in doing wrong and rejoice in the perverseness of evil, whose paths are crooked and who are devious in their ways.
>
> Proverbs 2:1–15

Proverbs is full of teaching about wisdom. In chapter 2, wisdom is seen as a guardian from evil and a protector that guides us away from the deceptive detours that lead to destruction. Cherished one, you and I must be wise women in the midst of a dark world if we are going to live pure lives for Jesus Christ. Wisdom applies the truth we have learned thus far and makes good judgments. As James 1:22 says, "Do not merely listen to the word, and so deceive yourselves. Do what it says." We must apply the truth and live it out.

Now that you know God's design for sex, the reality of the spiritual war around and within you, and why you are fighting, I pray you will make wise choices to achieve your goal. A cherished woman must choose to walk in wisdom in order to experience God's best.

> It is God's will that you should be sanctified: that you should avoid sexual immorality; that each of you should learn to control your own body in a way that is holy and honorable, not in passionate lust like the pagans, who do not know God.
>
> 1 Thessalonians 4:3–5

This verse teaches that in order to avoid sexual immorality, we must learn to "control" our fleshly impulses in order to honor God. As I battled for sexual purity, God led me by His Spirit to make specific wise choices concerning dating and relationships. God's wisdom led me to establish boundaries, abstain from activities, say no to certain pursuers, and avoid evil. I did not see these choices as "legalistic rules" but as applied wisdom. Our Enemy is crafty; defeating him would require me to apply the Word of God directly to everyday circumstances.

Speak Up!

Cherished ones, the first thing you must do is decide today, right now, what your emotional and physical boundaries are prior to marriage. Then be prepared to share these with any man who pursues you. This first step is absolutely necessary. Once feelings are involved and chemistry starts cooking, it is way too late to establish your physical boundaries. In the heat of the moment, it is impossible to have a rational conversation with a guy about your desire to honor God through sexual purity.

Justin and I actually talked about our mutual desire to honor God by abstaining from sex until marriage long before our first date! As we were getting to know each other via emails and phone calls, Jesus was at the forefront of our conversation. I can't even remember who spoke up first, but I know that it was clear where we both stood on sexual purity well before he opened my car door for our first date.

How do you do this? What I recommend to girls I mentor is this: Speak up! Just be frank and tell the guy you need to discuss something very important with him. Explain to him that you believe God says you are cherished and that sex is for marriage *only*. Let him know your expectations when it comes to dating and physical boundaries. I know some of you may be thinking, *Isn't the guy supposed to lead?* Sure, that would be nice, but you are not stepping out of line by initiating the conversation. You are a priceless treasure, and if you expect a man to treat you the way God desires for you to be treated, then you must speak up. And if this scares him off, then get up and do a little happy dance that God protected you from such a creeper!

How Far Is Too Far?

Now I face the moment that all writers of purity books must face. I must address the question of "How far is too far?" The physical boundary that Justin and I established in our relationship was this: Anything beyond kissing prior to marriage was off-limits. There was only one base for us, and that was first base. But I must be honest. What we came to realize is this: Kissing is dangerous. Kissing opens the door to sexual temptation and makes it very difficult to remain pure. Even though we didn't cross this line, we struggled. In order to not fall into sin, we had to reestablish our boundaries from time to time.

Concerning sexual purity and physical boundaries, author Randy Alcorn writes:

> There is a continuum of physical contact that begins with things like sitting close and hand-holding on the near side and moves to sexual intercourse on the far side. In between might be an arm around the shoulder, a brief hug, a kiss on the cheek, a kiss on the mouth, a longer hug, prolonged kissing, fondling, etc. Scripture does not spell out exactly what "intermediate" behavior is permissible, but one thing is certain—the line must be drawn before either of you becomes sexually stimulated. This means that fondling—and anything else that results in a "turn on"—is forbidden.[3]

The beautiful thing about purity is how your relationship can blossom and grow deeper when the physical aspect doesn't dominate. I would encourage you to consider waiting as long as possible before introducing a kiss into a relationship. Several friends of mine waited until their wedding day and it was the most romantic thing ever!

Another good friend of mine gave me this advice when I was a new Christian and trying to understand sexual purity: "Keep the small things sacred." By that she meant that holding hands should be a really big deal. A gentle kiss on the cheek at the end of the night will make a girl swoon. The last level of intimacy that is permissible is a kiss prior to marriage. Most people start with the kiss and then struggle to stay pure, but when the kiss is the last thing introduced, the fight is not nearly as difficult.

When speaking of communicating physical boundaries, this next statement should go without saying, but I realize in our culture that it cannot. I must say this because many Christian women have been deceived into believing that spending the night together is acceptable if sex is not involved. This is a major issue. For starters, Scripture is clear: "Marriage should be honored by all, and the marriage bed kept pure, for God will judge the adulterer and all the sexually immoral" (Hebrews 13:4).

Girls, God says to "Keep the marriage bed pure." This means that marriage is holy in the eyes of the Lord, and that sharing the intimacy of a bed with someone is reserved for the covenant spouse. I believe this to mean that a man and woman should not share the same bed until they are man and wife. The marriage bed is sacred, and when we share this privilege with anyone other than our husbands, we are not honoring the "marriage bed."

No shacking up! No slumber parties! I know those are so tempting, and the little voice in your head says, "It's no big deal. I just want to cuddle." But to the Lord, it is a very big deal. Establishing this boundary early on will keep you from so many temptations and will profoundly bless your future marriage. Save all those snuggles for your hubby!

Make No Provision for the Flesh!

An eye-opening Scripture that is packed with wisdom for winning the battle for sexual purity is Romans 13:14, which says, "Put on the Lord Jesus Christ, and make no provision for the flesh in regard to its lusts" (NASB). I recall reading this passage in my quiet time one day and pausing over the words *make no provision*. I knew the Lord was revealing an important truth, so I stopped to ponder these words:

MAKE ... NO ... PROVISION.

To "make provision" implies forethought, planning, or preparation. When it comes to sin, sometimes we slip up and say "oops," and other times we willingly walk into situations that set us up for failure. This happens all the time with believers when it comes to sexual sin. We may desire purity, but we willingly put ourselves in vulnerable situations that entice our flesh and make us weak to Satan's lies. The following are a few danger zones:

Dating a Non-Christian

Although the Bible explicitly states that we are not to marry someone who does not follow Christ, many women date men who are not Christians. This is a big danger zone! Randy Alcorn gives this nugget of wisdom concerning dating nonbelievers:

> Dating is the path to marriage. You will not marry every person you date. But the person you marry will be someone you dated. Therefore every date is a potential mate. If you wouldn't marry a person because they don't know Christ, that's a good enough reason not to date them. More young men and women are derailed from their walk with Christ by dating nonbelievers than anything else. The longer you allow a relationship to go on with a nonbeliever, the more cloudy your judgment will become and the more likely you will commit immorality and turn your back on the Lord in other ways. Convictions waver when we place ourselves in the realm of temptation. There is only one way to be sure you do not marry an unbeliever: never date an unbeliever.[4]

Sexual purity is hard enough for two committed Christians, but when you willingly date someone who does not love God, you are fighting a losing battle. This man will not honor your purity or seek to treat you as Christ would, because he does not share your same love for God or your same values.

Alone Time

Some of you reading this may be in high school and you have built-in chaperones (i.e., the 'rents). For the rest of you, who are either in college or living as independent single women, you don't have the built-in protection of watching eyes to help in winning the battle for purity.

Girls, I'm going to say it again. God's best is worth fighting for! One way we fight is by establishing our own boundaries and curfews so we don't make provision for our flesh.

One thing I realized early on in my pursuit of purity is that my flesh could not be trusted. I knew, given the right set of circumstances, my flesh would sin. After all, as we discussed in the previous chapter, our flesh loves sin. Therefore, we must guard against providing it an opportunity.

One of the best ways to make "no provision for the flesh" is to limit alone time. You may think this advice sounds crazy and super old-school, but hear me out. I know your adorable boyfriend is who you want to spend every second of your time with. I get it. But make sure those moments together are redemptive and not destructive. A wise woman will take the time to plan activities that don't revolve around a couch (if you know what I mean!). The reward for being intentional is amazing!

Redeem the Time

In the moment of strength, make decisions that will avoid temptation in the moment of weakness. When you're on a diet, don't step foot in a doughnut shop. In fact, don't even walk down the street the doughnut shop's on. [5]

When Justin and I were dating, we had a motto: "Redeem the time." We intentionally planned activities so that we would not just sit around each other's houses fighting the temptation to make out. We went to painting classes, we went mountain biking, we trained for a marathon, we took cooking classes, and we planned events with friends. We intentionally focused our time on building our friendship.

Today, I know this was the best decision ever! Honestly, we are best friends. Here's the truth: The physical aspect of a relationship is super easy. The physical will be there once you say "I do." What is difficult for most couples is communication, finding activities you both enjoy, and building a friendship that will last a lifetime. Dating is the best time to learn these things and to develop communication that involves more than wandering hands! *Redeem the time!* When you focus on building your friendship, you are laying a foundation that will last a lifetime.

The opposite principle also proves true. Couples who indulge their flesh before marriage typically find that, months and years later, they don't know how to communicate and they don't really have much in common because the physical aspect of their relationship was the priority while dating. Whenever the physical is the focus of a relationship, all other aspects suffer.

Before I move on to the next tip, I need to address one of the biggest ways Christians make provision for the flesh during alone time.

It's dark.

It's cozy.

It's movie night.

This one seems so very innocent, but one of the biggest ways we can make provision for our flesh is when we are alone on the couch, "watching" a movie together. You cuddle up to watch your favorite romantic comedy, and the next thing you know, the heat is on! One simple little kiss turns into a full-on make-out session!

Most of my solid Christian friends have confessed to me that the time they struggled the very most was when sitting on the couch watching a movie. I know this is a hard suggestion, but I would highly recommend not watching movies alone. Invite a group. Make it a party. Just don't let your flesh deceive you into thinking you can handle the temptation. Let me remind you, your flesh will lie to you. It will deceive you. It cannot be trusted.

Accountability

The Christian life is meant for community. God did not expect us to fly solo. We are called the body of Christ for a reason. As members of His body, we are in fellowship and community to help one another love and serve God. From the time I became a Christian in my mid-twenties, I have been involved in an accountability group with women who love Jesus and who desire to live for His glory. We have seen each other through all of life's stages: dating, marriage, babies, and everything in between.

Not only have I loved meeting with these women over the years, I've desperately needed it. Why? Oh, the answer is super easy . . . because I do not trust my flesh for one hot second. The apostle Paul writes in Philippians 3:3 that we are to "put no confidence in the flesh." This is a good word for a cherished woman to apply. Our flesh is not to be trusted. It will lie to us. It will deceive us. The flesh will detour us faster than you can imagine.

Confidence in the flesh is walking into a situation and thinking, *Oh, I'm fine. Nothing is going to happen. I'm beyond temptation.* A good dose of humility would do all of us some good. We must remind ourselves daily that our sinful nature is capable of anything! We must be humble enough to admit that we need help and to acknowledge our struggles with people who care for us. God's Word says, "So, if you think you are standing firm, be careful that you don't fall!" (1 Corinthians 10:12). Any of us are able, at any time, to fall into sin.

In winning the battle for sexual purity, accountability is simply inviting other women who love Jesus to speak truth into your life, to ask you tough questions and to pray for you in moments of weakness. Without a doubt, I would not have made it without accountability.

My girlfriends knew the specific ways the Enemy would lie to me and were quick to counter those lies with God's truth. My friends were on speed dial to pray for me to stand strong in the face of temptation. I even had one friend who would call me at 10 p.m. just to "check in."

Justin and I surrounded ourselves with accountability because we did not want to fall for Satan's schemes. Since we dated long distance, there was plenty of opportunity for temptation and deception. God provided a Christian family in San Antonio for me to stay with when I would visit. This godly couple was part of our accountability covering. They knew when I came home every night and were available when we needed prayer.

If you don't currently have these types of relationships, then pray and ask God for them. As a single woman, this season of your life is the best time to cultivate godly Christian friendships. One of the very first prayers I wrote in my prayer journal years ago was asking God to provide Christian friends. (For more on this topic, read my book *The Girlfriends Guidebook*.)

Don't Feed the Flesh

Just two weeks prior to my wedding day, I sat in a hair salon flipping through magazines, looking at bridal hairstyles while I waited for my appointment. Justin and I had finished all of our premarital counseling and wedding showers, and we were counting down the days until we would be husband and wife.

Girls, for the record, fighting for purity during engagement requires a whole new level of discipline. At this point, you are beginning to feel like "one," and that shiny new diamond on your left hand sparkles and gleams so bright that it almost

seems true. For this reason, I HIGHLY RECOMMEND A VERY
SHORT ENGAGEMENT. Let me repeat. A. VERY. SHORT.
ENGAGEMENT! Don't set yourself up for trouble. You can
plan a fabulous wedding in less than six months. Mine was
flat-out amazing and we planned it in three. "Just get thyself
married" is my motto.

Back to the hair salon.

While waiting for my appointment, I flipped through a well-
known women's magazine and landed on an article about sex.
Since I was less than two weeks away from my honeymoon,
I figured I should read the advice the magazine offered. To
quote Julia Roberts's famous line from *Pretty Woman*, "Big
mistake. . . . Huge!"

At first I naïvely thought reading the article was "no big deal,"
but then as I continued to read, the editorial became more ex-
plicit and graphic. Embarrassed that I would be found reading
it, I slipped the magazine down and hid it behind my enormous
purse. Obviously, I knew it was wrong. Something inside me
whispered, "Don't read this." But I ignored the voice of wisdom
and kept on reading, telling myself that a married woman would
need to know these things.

Later that night, I met up with Justin for a rare dinner
date in the midst of engagement frenzy. I am so embarrassed
to admit this, but as we shared fajitas and talked about last-
minute wedding details, the words and the images from the
article paraded through my mind. My flesh was so tempted,
and I had to silently pray to the Lord, "Help me!" My spirit was
willing but my flesh was weak. My flesh had grown stronger
that day because I had fed it. (Remember the two puppies?
The one you feed grows!)

Cherished ones, we must grasp the power of this truth: *Whatever fills us, controls us.* If we fill our minds with sexual images,
those images will control our thoughts. Beware of anything that

incites lust. When we watch movies with sexual scenes or read books with erotic content, we are feeding our flesh.

Remember the old saying, "Garbage in, garbage out"? If we fill our minds with books, magazines, and movies loaded with sexuality, then we inevitably adopt the morality of the programs. Randy Alcorn gives this wise counsel when he writes:

> Actions, habits, character and destiny all start with a thought, and thoughts are fostered by what we choose to take into our minds. Therefore we should take extreme care about what we feed our minds on.[6]

Even though we live in a rom-com world, we must be very careful about what we choose to watch, read, or listen to. Psalm 119:37 says, "Turn my eyes away from worthless things; preserve my life according to your word."

Speaking of turning our eyes from worthless things, I must stop and address the epidemic of pornography. The onslaught of sexual images via media and the Internet is a direct attack of the Enemy on a woman's heart, mind, and soul . . . not to mention her future marriage.

Our culture has twisted and perverted God's beautiful design for sex. Instead of finding fulfillment as God designed, Satan has offered a counterfeit that has millions in captivity. This prison is called pornography. Men are not alone in this struggle. Thirty-four percent of female readers of *Today's Christian Woman* admitted to "intentionally accessing Internet porn." One out of every six women who read *Today's Christian Woman* say they struggle with addiction to pornography.[7]

Crystal Renaud, author of *Dirty Girls Come Clean*, said in an interview with ABC News, "Women are also visually stimulated and are attracted to pornography in many of the same ways as men are. But what makes women and women's use of pornography all the more destructive and potentially dangerous is our innate desire for emotional connection." Pornography is "affordable, accessible and anonymous," according to Renaud, and eventually can become a substitute for a relationship.[8]

Women of all ages and stages of life face temptations to meet legitimate needs in illegitimate ways. I would suggest that one of Satan's most deadly detours is the path of pornography. If you find yourself struggling with this specific temptation, seek immediate help. Find a biblical counselor who can address the core issues that led to this destructive habit and who can direct you in meeting the emotional needs at the core of the temptation. Our Enemy loves to operate in darkness, yet our freedom is found when the darkness is exposed by the light of God's truth and grace.

Just as what we choose to feed our bodies affects how we look and feel, so does what we choose to fill our minds with affect us . . . body, mind, soul, and spirit. Throughout this book, we have learned the power of our thoughts and how our minds are the battleground upon which the war for our souls is fought. Cherished ones, we must be on guard and not give our Enemy access to our lives through our minds. This means we are women who choose wisely the books we read, the websites we visit, and the movies we watch.

Fasting

Another way to deny the flesh power to rule over you is through fasting. Fasting can take many forms—a fast from food, television, social media, etc.—but the purpose or heart of the fast is to draw closer to Jesus and pray. When we intentionally deny ourselves something in order to use that time to draw closer to God, our old sinful nature is resisted and, in other words, starved. Spiritual fasting is not just about giving up food or some other pleasure but about feeding our spirit through our obedience to God.

One fast that I would highly recommend to any woman who is struggling with sexual purity is a boy fast or a dating fast. Yep, you read that right. I think it is a great idea for a woman who is a little too boy crazy to take some time to step back, examine her heart and weaknesses, and draw near to Jesus. (A dating fast is not just for those struggling with sexual sin. It can be super beneficial to any woman wanting to grow closer to Christ.)

Why would I recommend this type of fast? First of all, we often need time to unlearn old behaviors. For instance, if in the past you have related to men in a way that did not honor God, then your flesh only knows one way to interact with men. You need to take some time to step back and allow the Holy Spirit to cleanse you, heal you, and renew your mind.

For those of you who want to throw this book across the room, I get it. But take a deep breath. I'm not asking you to run away to a convent and become a nun. I'm simply saying that taking a break from guys (for a season) is not a bad idea. It could be six weeks or six months.

The first few years after becoming a Christian, I rarely dated. In some ways this was not my choice. Looking back, I think the Lord hid me from men's eyes in order to protect me and to renew my purity. So without really meaning to, I was on a God-imposed dating fast. During those years, I grew spiritually by leaps and bounds, and my heart radically changed. Purity became the goal. I learned to relate to men as my brothers in Christ, I learned to walk in the power of the Spirit, but most of all, I fell head over heels in love with Jesus Christ.

> *To fall in love with God is the greatest of all romances;*
> *To seek him, the greatest adventure;*
> *To find him, the greatest human achievement.*
> *—Augustine*

The best love is the kind that awakens the soul
and makes us reach for more, that plants a fire
in our hearts and brings peace to our minds,
and that's what you've given me.

~ Noah (Ryan Gosling)
in *The Notebook*

Conclusion

Jesus is better!

We are not called to focus on the battle or the devil . . . our calling is to focus on Jesus. The work of the devil, however, is to draw our eyes from Jesus. Satan's first weapon always involves luring our eyes from Christ.

—Francis Frangipane, *The Three Battlegrounds*

I desperately wanted to make a beeline for the exit and detour. When I saw the exit sign for the 5K runners, I was doing okay, but once I reached the 10K mark, everything in me wanted to turn right and follow the pack leaving the official race course. The 10K mark in my first half marathon was my official breaking point.

As previously confessed, I'm not a naturally gifted runner. Off and on since high school, I've picked up jogging for the sheer fact that I like food way too much. But I've never been one of those gals who wakes up at the crack o' dawn bursting with enthusiasm about her morning jog.

I wish.

Honestly, before signing up for a half marathon, I would probably max out at four miles. I was actually shocked that no one gave me a jersey for such a feat. I even thought about putting one of those stickers on my car that says "4 miles," but I thought that would make all the other joggers jealous of my fierce athletic prowess.

Now that you know my not-so-amazing running history, you can appreciate how challenging it was for me to run 13.1 miles. Sometime around August of last year, one of my favorite ministries recruited me to run in the Houston Half Marathon in support of rescuing young girls out of sex trafficking. I tried to think of ways I could respectfully decline, but honestly, how does one say *no* to sex-trafficking rescue? Besides, an added benefit is the recommendation of "carbing-up." For this gluten-free gal, a free pass at carbs for a worthy cause put the butter on my bread, so to speak. I committed.

When I started training it was 106 degrees in Houston. Insanity is another name for training in Houston humidity. So for the first few weeks, I actually thought I was running in Hades. Slowly but surely, I began to build up mileage. Two miles turned to four. Four turned to six.

I guess I should mention that I was dating my husband at the time. Justin is what I call a gazelle. He, unlike yours truly, was built for running. Long legs. Hollow bones. He's the type of person non-runners hate. He actually smiles the whole time. It is super annoying. He runs thirteen miles for kicks on a Tuesday. So when I signed up for *the half*, he agreed to run with me. (Although he didn't need the months of training.)

Race day.

Before that morning, my max had been nine miles. (Side note: My training partners thought it was ten, but I found a way to walk and loop back through, and they were never the wiser.) In my defense, I was told that I didn't need to actually run the full

13.1 before race day because the endorphins and adrenaline would carry me through. So the ten-mile final run seemed like overkill. I got this . . . right? (SO NOT TRUE! COMPLETELY FALSE! NOT AT ALL REALITY!)

It was a warm, muggy October morning in Houston, dripping with humidity. Our team gathered at the starting line and joined thousands ready to pound the concrete for a few hours. Yes, I said hours. When I calculated my per-mile average and the distance of the race, I braced myself for the fact that I would be running for well over two hours. How depressing it is to realize that some people actually finish full marathons in that same amount of time. But I digress.

At first it wasn't so bad. I sang along to the worship music on my iPod. It was fun to see friends at the water stations who came to cheer us on. I progressed from miles one to six without a glitch. But then the pain hit. I began to slow down. The arches of my feet screamed from pounding the concrete streets. Then my side began to throb. I didn't realize it at the time, but I had started out running too fast in order to keep up with the other racers, so by mile six the extra exertion caught up with me. I had trained at a much slower pace, and my body started to revolt.

Right about that time, half of the people around me started to detour. Ahead of me was an exit marked "10K runners turn here." I can't tell you how tempting that exit appeared. No more pain. No more running. No more screaming arches. No more aching side. Visions of brunch danced through my head. EVERYTHING IN ME WANTED TO DETOUR!

Sensing my weakening will, Justin jogged beside me, smiling from ear to ear, and asked, "How's it going?" Teeth gritted, I barked, "Fine!" Then he started cheering me on. Bless his heart, I wanted to smack him. But then he did the best thing for me. He said, "I'm going to run right in front of you. All you need to do is put one foot in front of the other, and keep in pace with me. Don't look around, don't think about quitting, don't watch the other runners, just keep your eyes on me and I'll run you in."

I could almost cry thinking about it.

For the next six miles, he did just that. He ran right in front of me so that I could match his steps. When tempted to slow down or quit, I looked up, saw him in front of me, and put one foot in front of the other, all the way to the finish line. I kept telling myself, "Don't quit. Keep your eyes on Justin. Run."

About a mile from the finish line, the spiritual truth smacked me harder in the face than my feet hitting the pavement. The Lord was teaching me that the secret to finishing the race is where you fix your eyes!

During my half marathon, I was tempted to quit. I wanted to detour. I wanted to sit down at the water station and stay there. But I didn't. The only way I crossed that finish line, running every step of the way, was by fixing my eyes.

The Bible doesn't sugarcoat the Christian life. It is a marathon. It is not a sprint. Purity is a lifelong pursuit without a finish line. Whether married or single, we will face temptations to detour, but we must press on. Why? Our purity in the midst of an impure world is an act of worship unto Jesus. Purity is not defined by our relationship status. Purity is about exalting Jesus as better.

> Therefore, since we are surrounded by such a great cloud of witnesses, let us throw off everything that hinders and the sin that so easily entangles. And let us run with perseverance the race marked out for us, fixing our eyes on Jesus, the pioneer and perfecter of faith. For the joy set before him he endured the cross, scorning its shame, and sat down at the right hand of the throne of God.
>
> Hebrews 12:1–2

One translation says, "Fix your eyes on Jesus." Dear sisters, as we conclude this book, I hope you see that this is the ultimate key to a life of sexual purity. Keep your eyes on Jesus. When we behold Him, Satan's temptations and detours lose their luster.

Look unto Jesus, the One who endured the suffering and pain of the cross with His eyes fixed on His future glory. The One who, with outstretched arms, said you are "worth dying for." The One who endured humiliation with His gaze set on redemption. Cherished ones, keep your eyes on Jesus, for He is better. This is the driving ambition of our souls—to proclaim Jesus as glorious. As Søren Kierkegaard said, "Purity of heart is to will one thing." For the cherished woman, our "one thing" is Jesus. His fame is our one pure and holy passion.

I can't make you an empty promise that if you follow a formula you will find happily ever after. I wouldn't dare do that to you.

I can, however, promise you this: If you run hard after Jesus, you will never regret it. He is the goal of our purity. We aren't pursuing Jesus in order to gain something, for in Him we have everything.

My goal in this book has been to equip you to resist an invisible Enemy who wants to steal, kill, and destroy your life. My great hope at the conclusion of this book is that more than anything, you will run hard after Jesus, for He is better.

Recommended Resources

To Find a Christian Counselor in Your Area

- American Association of Christian Counselors
  www.aacc.net

Recommended Books

- *Sex and the City Uncovered: Exposing the Emptiness and Healing the Hurt* by Marian Jordan
- *Sex and the Soul of a Woman: How God Restores the Beauty of Relationships from the Pain of Regret* by Paula Rinehart
- *Victory Over the Darkness: Realize the Power of Your Identity in Christ* by Neil T. Anderson

For Women Struggling With Same-Sex Attraction

- *Restoring Sexual Identity* by Anne Paulk

For Women Struggling With Pornography

- Covenant Eyes Ministry, www.covenanteyes.com
- *Dirty Girls Come Clean* by Crystal Renaud

For Victims of Sexual Abuse

- *No Place to Cry: The Hurt and Healing of Sexual Abuse* by Doris Van Stone and Erwin W. Lutzer
- *The Wounded Heart: Hope for Adult Victims of Childhood Sexual Abuse* by Dan B. Allender

Small-Group Questions

Introduction

1. What is your favorite romantic comedy? Why?

2. Why do you think romantic comedies are so appealing to women?

3. In the introduction, Marian writes, "It can be a tough world for a godly girl. We live in a culture that sells sex, promotes sex, and degrades sex, yet God calls His daughters to live as light in this darkness."

   How does our culture (books, magazines, movies, TV, celebrities, friends, parents, etc.) make it difficult for you to follow God and pursue purity?

4. On page 15, Marian writes, "Perhaps you've *Never Been Kissed*, or maybe you're the girl with *27 Dresses*, or maybe your life looks more like a scene from *Knocked Up*. Wherever you are on this journey, this book is for you."

   If your life were a romantic comedy, what would be the title?

Chapter One

1. In this chapter, Marian uses a strong phrase to describe her single/dating years by calling them a war zone. Why do you think she used this term? Can you relate?

2. Marian writes, "My single years were a faith walk—to trust in God's promises and to resist the lies and schemes of the Enemy."

   Has your faith in God ever been tested? When have you struggled to believe His promises?

3. How does this chapter define purity?

4. On page 25, Marian describes being "consecrated" to the Lord. What does this mean? What would this look like in real life?

5. How does a love for Jesus compel someone to live a life of sexual purity?

Chapter Two

1. Marian writes,

   > Intrinsic to a woman's nature is the longing for covenant love. There's a reason women flock to romantic comedies and little girls dress up as their favorite fairy-tale princesses—our souls were fashioned by a God who loves us sacrificially, who says we are worth fighting for. This love story is inscribed upon our very souls. For so many women, a wedding is about this fairy tale coming to life.

   Discuss a woman's intrinsic desire for sacrificial, covenant love.

   How have you seen this desire in your own life?

2. Marian writes,

   > Traditional wedding vows contain three simple yet profoundly beautiful tokens of devotion: The groom stands

before God and witnesses at an altar—biblically known as a place of sacrifice—and commits to lay down his life in order to love, honor, and cherish His bride. This vow stands as a picture to the watching world of what Christ did for His bride, the church. The Christian wedding vow is based in Scripture, where God reveals the mystery that Jesus' sacrificial love is the model for Christian marriage.

Read aloud Ephesians 5:25–32 and discuss what Jesus did for His bride, the church.

3. Define the word *cherish* based on what you learned in this chapter.

4. What is something that you cherish?

5. Marian writes,

> Jesus willingly went to the cross to die . . . for you. He experienced unbelievable suffering and shame all with one purpose in mind: to rescue you. As Ephesians 5:25–26 plainly states, "Husbands, love your wives, just as Christ loved the church and gave himself up for her." That's you and that's me—the bride of Christ. He "gave himself up" for us. Jesus' sacrificial love defines the word *cherished* and stands as God's expectation for how a man should treat one of His daughters. Stop and really read that Scripture. Pause. Believe. The God of the universe said with outstretched arms that you were "worth dying for." Believing this truth transforms everything. . . .

How does your heart respond to the phrase "worth dying for"?

Chapter Three

1. In the opening statement of this chapter, Marian writes, "Ignorance is not bliss; it proves to be downright dangerous." How have you seen this truth play out in your own life?

2. In this chapter, Marian confesses:

> I knew temptation is a reality all believers face, but honestly, I just assumed that if I loved Jesus and wanted to walk in purity, then I would be fine. My heart desired to remain sexually pure for my husband and for the glory of God. Therefore, I assumed my good intentions would carry me through to my wedding day. I quickly learned that good intentions aren't always good enough. I didn't realize the sheer power of temptation. I didn't realize that Satan's schemes are tactical. He knew my insecurities, he knew my fears, and he knew my weaknesses. Unbeknownst to me, I was facing a strategic move by a cunning Enemy who seeks "to kill and steal and destroy" (John 10:10), and who will use any means or method to accomplish his mission.

Read aloud John 10:10. What does Jesus offer and what does Satan desire to do?

Read aloud 1 Corinthians 10:12–13. What warning is given in this Scripture?

3. Discuss the statement "Good intentions aren't always good enough." Share a time when "good intentions" were not enough to resist Satan's schemes.

4. What is spiritual warfare, according to this chapter?

5. How does "falling in love" numb us to the reality of spiritual warfare and the schemes of the Enemy?

6. Marian confesses her intense battle with temptation when she writes,

> Purity, born out of love for Jesus, proved to be a war fought on three battlegrounds: a world system opposed to God, an ancient foe who hates God and His glory, and my own ugly sinful nature. While my heart longed to live for God's glory and experience His highest and best, I was a girl living in Enemy-occupied territory. The war raged both around me and within me. Although my heart wanted to

honor Jesus with sexual purity, I've never experienced a greater struggle with temptation in my entire life.

Can you relate to her struggle?

7. Read 1 Peter 2:11. How is sexual temptation a type of spiritual warfare?

8. How did this chapter change your perspective on abstaining from sexual sin? Explain.

Chapter Four

1. Why is a "purity ring" not enough to protect a woman from sexual sin?

2. Read the following passage and discuss.

> Satan flat-out hates marriage. He despises a covenant built upon a vow to "love, honor, and cherish," because a biblical marriage is a picture of Christ's sacrificial love for His church. He especially hates God's glory—and love, sex, and marriage are all designed to perfectly reflect our glorious covenant relationship with God. . . . So Satan unleashed a full-fledged war against marriage. This war results in countless casualties: broken hearts, broken dreams, and broken promises. Satan begins his assault on a marriage covenant long before a girl even meets her future husband.

3. Why does Satan hate marriage?

4. Read and discuss Ephesians 6:10–14. Is spiritual warfare an option for Christians?

5. Have you experienced the battle Marian describes in this chapter?

If you aren't presently experiencing this struggle, how does this teaching prepare you for the battle you may encounter in the future?

6. Marian concludes this chapter with a challenge to be part of "the resistance of the cherished ones." What does this mean to you? What would this look like in your life?

Chapter Five

1. Read Proverbs 29:18. Why does Marian say vision is essential to sexual purity?

2. Discuss the statement "Rules will be broken, but visions are lived."

   How is this perspective a game changer when it comes to sexual purity?

3. How are God's commandments concerning sexual purity for our good and for our protection?

4. Marian writes,

   > While we live in a romantic-comedy world, which depicts sex as merely a recreational activity, God's message is that sex is a profound mystery, a glorious union between a man and a woman where two become one.

   Read aloud 1 Corinthians 6:16–18 (THE MESSAGE). How is God's design for sex different from what our culture promotes?

5. How is sex more than just a physical activity? What is a soul tie?

6. Why is God's best "worth waiting for"?

7. Share some examples of how the "world has made common what God made sacred."

8. Read the following excerpt:

   > Friends, as Christ-followers today, we, too, are living in our own kind of Babylon. For we also bear the name of God; we are His. And yet we live in a world that wants to

conform us to its ways. Sexual promiscuity is the norm
for those who do not know God, but it is not for the cherished daughters of the King. Like Shadrach, Meshach,
and Abednego, we are bombarded by the constant onslaught of media—image after image, scene after scene,
line after line. The worldview imprints upon our minds
and we begin to see the world's values as "normal" and
"acceptable." Through this indoctrination, Christian
women are tempted to adopt a radically different worldview from that of the Bible—a worldview that disregards
God, a worldview that degrades women, a worldview that
cheapens sex, and a worldview that enslaves us to sin.

What does Marian mean when she writes in this chapter,
"A woman of vision chooses to stand"?

9. How have you felt pressured to compromise your values
or standards of sexual purity?

Chapter Six

1. In this chapter, Marian teaches that God has a glorious
plan for our lives but that Satan also has an agenda. What
is his agenda? (See John 10:10.)

2. Read Matthew 7:13–14 and review the diagram on page
95. What is a "detour"?

Describe a few ways our Enemy can "steal, kill, or destroy."

3. In this chapter, Marian writes:

As we walk this narrow way, we will face temptations or
tempting detours that seem like quick and easy shortcuts
to our hearts' desire. These detours are Satan's schemes
to turn us away from the abundant life. To clarify, while
the Enemy knows we can never lose our salvation or our
standing as children of God, he does have a clear agenda.
Jesus spelled it out plainly for us in John 10:10: "The
thief came only to steal and kill and destroy."

How does he tempt us to turn away from the abundant life in Christ? Detours begin with the temptation to meet a legitimate need in an illegitimate way. Temptation whispers, "See this shortcut? If you turn here, you will reach the desire of your heart so much faster than taking that narrow road." Many travel the narrow road unaware of the deceptive detours along the path, only to realize they've been deceived after careening off the cliff.

Share some examples of "detours" you've taken from the narrow way in your spiritual journey.

What "orange cones" did you ignore along the way? What did you learn from that experience?

4. Reread the detour testimony shared in this chapter (pages 97–101). How was this woman tempted to meet a "legitimate need in an illegitimate way"?

5. Read Deuteronomy 30:15–20. When fighting for sexual purity, what does it mean to "choose life"?

Chapter Seven

1. In this chapter, Marian reviews "game film" of our Enemy. Why is it essential to know how our Enemy operates?

2. Who is Satan? What other names is he called? What is his primary mode of operation?

3. What was the cause of Satan's fall from heaven, according to Isaiah 14?

4. Describe how Satan uses doubt to lead us away from God.

5. Read Proverbs 3:5–6 and this excerpt.

This verse speaks of authority. As God's children, we are called to trust Him and rely on His Word as our guide. This verse explicitly warns us not to "lean on [our] own understanding." Imagine someone with a broken leg leaning on a crutch. This image helps us understand what this proverb is calling us to do. To *lean* means to rely, to put your weight upon, or to rest. When we "lean on our own understanding," we are relying on what we feel or think to determine our decisions. Scripture warns us that when faced with choices or decisions, how we "feel" is not always the best indicator of what we should "do."

Why is it dangerous to trust in our feelings or emotions rather than God's Word?

What does God promise to do if we trust Him?

6. In temptation, our Enemy seeks to undermine our trust in the goodness and love of God. Why does he do this?

7. In what ways has Satan whispered doubts or deceptions into your ear?

Chapter Eight

1. How is temptation defined in this chapter? Did you discover anything about the nature of temptation that you had not considered before?

2. Why are our thoughts so powerful when it comes to sexual purity?

3. Marian shares seven common lies women believe that open the door for sexual sin. Briefly review and discuss each of these lies as a group.

4. Marian writes,

> I often ask young women, "Are you buying the lie or believing the truth?" One of the most pervasive lies women believe is that sex is a commodity that can be traded for love. This lie is absolutely ingrained in our culture. Girls from great families or women from broken pasts—it really doesn't make much of a difference—have believed the lie that sex will secure the love they crave.

Why do you think women so often believe the lie that sex will deliver the love their hearts crave?

5. These seven lies are exposed in order to reveal how our Enemy strategically targets a woman's insecurities and desires. Marian shared how Satan tempted her when she felt insecure about her weight. Share how temptation has targeted your own insecurity.

6. Marian listed seven common lies that women believe. Are there any other lies, besides the ones listed in this chapter, that you would add to this list? (Remember, a lie is anything that contradicts God's truth.)

Chapter Nine

1. In the opening section of this chapter, Marian discusses "the trade-off," how when Esau was famished, he traded his birthright for a bowl of stew. She goes on to say,

> This is also how sexual temptation works. When we are hungry—be that for love, affection, attention, affirmation, comfort, or belonging—our Enemy strikes. Cherished ones, I hope you will stop right now and take an honest look at your soul hunger. Don't sell your birthright as a cherished daughter of the King. A woman's fight for purity will always be a tough one if she is famished for affection. Dealing with these deeper issues is the key to victory.

What issues from your past (abuse, heartbreak, abandonment, etc.) are causing you to be famished for love and affection?

2. Read 1 Peter 5:8–9. What does it mean to "resist" the Enemy?

3. According to Matthew 4:1–11, how did Jesus resist Satan when He was tempted in the wilderness?

4. Marian writes,

> When we are hungry for love, acceptance, importance, recognition, or anything the human heart can desire, he tempts us to satisfy this hunger in a way that is disobedient to our heavenly Father. Think back to those seven lies we uncovered in the previous chapter. Each one strikes at a place of hunger in a woman's heart—our hunger for love, security, comfort, belonging, or acceptance. Behind each lie is the Enemy enticing us to meet our legitimate need in an illegitimate way.

   Where does Satan specifically target temptation? Share a time when you were "hungry" and experienced temptation.

5. What is "soul hunger," according to this chapter?

6. What is the sword of the Spirit, and how does a believer use it to resist our Enemy?

7. Read 2 Corinthians 10:3–5. How do we win the battle for our minds?

8. Which of the battle verses listed in this chapter do you need to commit to memory?

Chapter Ten

1. What new insights about the victorious Christian life did you glean from this chapter?

2. Who are you, according to 1 Corinthians 3:16? How does this truth change the way you see yourself?

3. What does it mean to "feed the flesh" or "feed the spirit"?

4. *Abide* means to fully rely on or remain connected to Jesus. In this chapter, Marian teaches the acronym D.A.I.L.Y. to explain how a woman can abide in Christ.

What does each letter represent? Discuss the need to abide daily in Jesus.

5. Read the following excerpt and discuss:

> During my daily quiet time, I ask Jesus to fill me with His Holy Spirit. This is a time of confessing my weaknesses and asking God to give me His strength. This prayer is twofold. First, I lay down my sin and struggles with my palms facing down. Then, as I ask God to fill me, I turn my palms upward and invite the Holy Spirit to empower me. This is not a magic formula, but I feel connected to the prayer when I add the physical movements to the requests.
>
> Sexual purity is one aspect of this empowering. While dating my husband, I would confess to God my weaknesses: my soul hunger for love, the lies that hounded my insecurities, and the various temptations. I would bring those thoughts and struggles to Christ. On my knees before God, I would lay those issues down. Then I would open up my palms and ask God to fill me with His Spirit. I would specifically ask for the strength to resist temptation. I would specifically ask for wisdom. I would specifically ask for His Spirit to increase in me so that I could say no to my flesh.

Why do we often hold back from confessing our weaknesses?

Why do we need to specifically ask for empowering?

6. Marian shares the acronym P.U.R.E. in this chapter for restoration of purity. Discuss each step as a group.

7. After his sexual sin of adultery, King David repented and penned Psalm 51. Take a few minutes as a group and read aloud this psalm. What does David confess? What does David ask God to do for him?

8. On page 175 of this chapter, Marian shares a prayer for breaking soul ties. First, read through the prayer as a group, and then pray with individuals who need to break free from their sexual past.

Chapter Eleven

1. What is the difference between wisdom and knowledge?

2. How does wisdom equip a woman to win the war for sexual purity?

3. Read 1 Thessalonians 4:3–5. What is God's will according to this passage? What must we learn to do?

4. Read the following excerpt:

   > Cherished ones, the first thing you must do is decide today, right now, what your emotional and physical boundaries are prior to marriage. Then be prepared to share these with any man who pursues you. This first step is absolutely necessary. Once feelings are involved and chemistry starts cooking, it is way too late to establish your physical boundaries. In the heat of the moment, it is impossible to have a rational conversation with a guy about your desire to honor God through sexual purity.

   As an accountability group, discuss and establish your physical boundaries.

5. Marian says, "Keep the small things sacred." Discuss practical ways to pursue purity.

6. What does it mean to "make no provision for the flesh"? Why is this important?

7. In this chapter, Marian shares the vital importance of accountability. Who is a godly influence in your life who will help hold you accountable to sexual purity?

Conclusion

1. How has your perspective on sex and fighting for purity changed since reading this book?

2. God says you are "cherished" and are "worth dying for." How does this truth change your perspective on sex before marriage?

3. Marian writes,

> The Bible doesn't sugarcoat the Christian life. It is a marathon, not a sprint. Purity is a lifelong pursuit without a finish line. Whether married or single, we will face temptations to detour, but we must press on. Why? Our purity in the midst of an impure world is an act of worship unto Jesus. Purity is not defined by our relationship status. Purity is about exalting Jesus as better.

What is your personal definition of purity?

4. Read Hebrews 12:1–2.

In this final chapter, Marian compares a marathon race to the long road of obedience in following God. What does she say is the ultimate goal? What keeps us from detouring?

5. Marian concludes with this statement:

> My goal in this book has been to equip you to resist an invisible Enemy who wants to steal, kill, and destroy your life. My great hope at the conclusion of this book is that more than anything, you will run hard after Jesus, for He is better.

As a group, share your personal commitments to pursuing Jesus and living for His glory.

Notes

Chapter 2: Cherish

1. C. S. Lewis, *Mere Christianity* (New York: Macmillan Publishing, 1978), 54.

Chapter 3: The War Against the Soul

1. Robert Jeffress, *The Divine Defense* (Colorado Springs: Waterbrook Press, 2006), 11.

Chapter 4: Good Intentions Aren't Good Enough

1. T. C. Muck, *Sins of the Body: Ministry in a Sexual Society* (Carol Stream, IL: Christianity Today, 1989), 118.
2. Stu Weber, *Spirit Warriors: Strategies for the Battles Christian Men and Women Face Every Day* (Sisters, OR: Multnomah, 2001), 8.
3. Kenneth Boa, *Conformed to His Image* (Grand Rapids: Zondervan, 2001), 89.
4. John and Stasi Eldredge, *Love and War* (Colorado Springs: WaterBrook, 2011), 38–39.

Chapter 5: Vision

1. *MacMillan Dictionary*, s.v. "vision," accessed July 26, 2013, http://www.macmillandictionary.com/dictionary/british/vision.
2. Paula Rinehart, *Sex and the Soul of a Woman* (Grand Rapids: Zondervan, 2004), 91.
3. Adapted from Marian Jordan, *Sex and the City Uncovered* (Nashville: B&H Publishing, 2007). Used by permission.
4. Ibid.
5. Ibid.
6. Ibid.

7. Erwin Lutzer, *Putting Your Past Behind You* (Chicago: Moody Press, 1990).

8. Floyd Hitchcock, *The March of Empires—Lectures on the Book of Daniel*, 1944.

Chapter 7: Know Thy Enemy

1. J. Dwight Pentecost, *Your Adversary, the Devil* (Grand Rapids: Zondervan, 1969), introduction.

2. Mary E. DeMuth, *Beautiful Battle: A Woman's Guide to Spiritual Warfare* (Eugene, OR: Harvest House Publishers, 2012), 22.

3. J. R. Vassar, "Spiritual Warfare," sermon, Apostles Church NYC, August 16, 2009, www.apostlesnyc.com/sermon/spiritual-warfare/.

4. Neil T. Anderson, *A Way of Escape: Freedom from Sexual Strongholds* (Eugene, OR: Harvest House Publishers, 1998), 64.

5. I learned a great deal about the three-phase plan of temptation from a sermon by Brian Schwertley, "The Temptation of Eve," www.reformedonline.com/view/reformedonline/eve.htm.

6. *Merriam-Webster*, s.v. "authority," accessed July 26, 2013, http://www.merriam-webster.com/dictionary/authority.

7. *Merriam-Webster*, s.v. "lean," accessed July 26, 2013, http://www.merriam-webster.com/dictionary/lean.

8. John MacArthur, *Ephesians* (Chicago: Moody Publishers, 1986), 359.

9. Sam Storms, *Pleasures Evermore: The Life-Changing Power of Enjoying God* (Colorado Springs: NavPress, 2000), 27.

Chapter 8: The Battleground

1. John MacArthur, "The Believer's Armor: God's Provision for Your Protection," (Sermon, Grace to You Ministries, 1989), www.gty.org/resources/positions/P14/The-Believers-Armor-Gods-Provision-for-Your-Protection.

2. Dallas Willard, *Renovation of the Heart* (Colorado Springs: NavPress, 2002), 100.

3. Donna Schillinger, "Premarital Sex Is a Big Rip-off," *Purity's Big Payoff/Premarital Sex Is a Big Rip-off* (book promotion website), accessed July 26, 2013, http://purityorpremaritalsex.wordpress.com/premarital-sex/.

4. Miriam Grossman, *Unprotected* (New York: Sentinel, 2006), 4.

5. Alice Fryling, "Why Wait for Sex? A Look at the Lies We Face," *Christianity Today*, October 3, 1986.

6. Erwin Raphael McManus, *Soul Cravings: An Exploration of the Human Spirit* (Nashville: Thomas Nelson, 2006), entry 7.

7. Hayley DiMarco, *Technical Virgin: How Far Is Too Far?* (Grand Rapids: Revell, 2006).

8. Jeffress, 78.

Chapter 9: The Resistance of the Cherished Ones

1. Jeffress, 88.

2. Oswald Chambers, *He Shall Glorify Me* (Fort Washington, PA: Christian Literature Crusade, 1965), 134.

3. John Piper, *Future Grace: The Purifying Power of Living by Faith* (Portland, OR: Multnomah Books, 1995).

4. Shannon Ethridge, *Every Woman's Battle* (Colorado Springs: Waterbrook Press, 2003), 75.

Chapter 10: Winning the Battle Within

1. Jerry Bridges, *The Pursuit of Holiness* (Colorado Springs: NavPress, 1996), 92.

2. John MacArthur, "What Is Biblical Repentance?", Grace to You, July 13, 2009, www.gty.org/resources/articles/a330.

Chapter 11: The Wise Woman Wins the War

1. GoodReads.com, Taylor Swift quotes, accessed July 26, 2013, http://www.goodreads.com/quotes/218163-when-i-was-a-little-girl-i-used-to-read.

2. Jerry Bridges, *The Practice of Godliness* (Colorado Springs: NavPress, 1996), 89.

3. Randy Alcorn, "Guidelines for Sexual Purity," January 28, 2010, www.epm.org/resources/2010/Jan/28/guidelines-sexual-purity/. Randy Alcorn is the author of *The Purity Principle* and director of Eternal Perspective Ministries, epm.org. Used by permission.

4. Ibid.

5. Ibid.

6. Ibid.

7. Ramona Richards, "Dirty Little Secret: Men Aren't the Only Ones Lured by Internet Porn," *Today's Christian Woman*, September 1, 2003.

8. Susan Donaldson James, "Christians Ignore Female Pornography Addicts, Until Now," May 10, 2011, http://abcnews.go.com/Health/dirty-girls-clean-women-addicted-pornography/story?id=13565446.

Marian Jordan Ellis is the founder of Redeemed Girl Ministries. Marian's powerful testimony of coming to brokenness and emptiness and her dynamic account of Jesus Christ's transforming love and grace permeates all of her writings and speaking engagements.

Whole in Christ and ready to tell any ear that will listen, Marian loves Jesus and has a passion for sharing the Gospel and teaching women God's Word.

Marian is a graduate of Southwestern Baptist Theological Seminary. She is also the author of *Sex and the City Uncovered*, *Wilderness Skills for Women*, *The List*, *Radiant*, and *The Girlfriends Guidebook*.

A Texas girl at heart, Marian now lives in San Antonio with her husband, Justin, and her two bonus boys, Andrew and Brenden. When Marian isn't writing or on the road traveling to ministry events, she loves cooking, spending time with friends, and mountain biking with the boys.

To learn more about Marian Jordan Ellis, visit her website at www.marianjordan.com. You can also follow Marian on Twitter @marianjordan.